SAMURAI DEEPER
KYO

Translator - Takako Maeda & Dan Danko
English Adaptation - Dan Danko
Retouch and Lettering - Miyuki Ishihara and Deron Bennett
Copy Editor - Carol Fox
Cover Layout - Aaron Suhr

Editor - Jake Forbes
Managing Editor - Jill Freshney
Production Coordinator - Antonio DePietro
Production Manager - Jennifer Miller, Mutsumi Miyazaki
Art Director - Matt Alford
Editorial Director - Jeremy Ross
VP of Production - Ron Klamert
President & C.O.O. - John Parker
Publisher & C.E.O. - Stuart Levy

Email: editor@TOKYOPOP.com

Come visit us online at www.TOKYOPOP.com

A  Manga

TOKYOPOP Inc.
5900 Wilshire Blvd. Suite 2000
Los Angeles, CA 90036

Samurai Deeper Kyo Vol. 4

ISBN: 1-59182-249-1

First TOKYOPOP® printing: December 2003

10 9 8 7 6 5 4 3 2 1

Printed in the USA

Vol. 4

by Akimine Kamijyo

Los Angeles • Tokyo • London

SAMURAI DEEPER KYO

TABLE OF CONTENTS

YUYA-SAN

SAMURAI DEEPER KYO

CHARACTER PROFILES

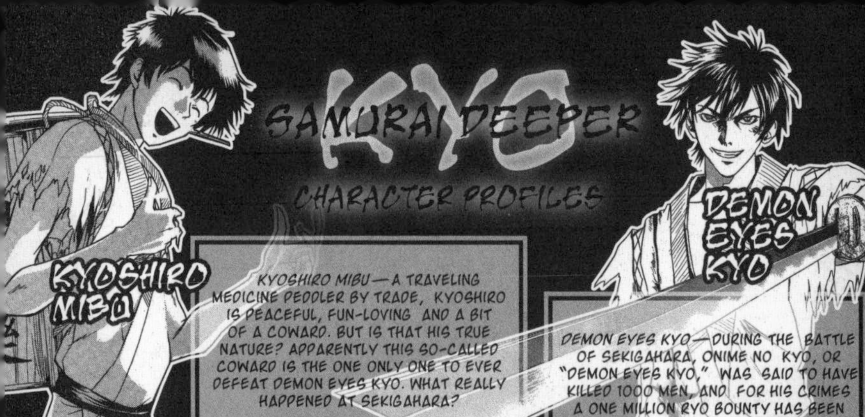

KYOSHIRO MIBU

KYOSHIRO MIBU—A TRAVELING MEDICINE PEDDLER BY TRADE, KYOSHIRO IS PEACEFUL, FUN-LOVING AND A BIT OF A COWARD. BUT IS THAT HIS TRUE NATURE? APPARENTLY THIS SO-CALLED COWARD IS THE ONE ONLY ONE TO EVER DEFEAT DEMON EYES KYO. WHAT REALLY HAPPENED AT SEKIGAHARA?

DEMON EYES KYO

DEMON EYES KYO—DURING THE BATTLE OF SEKIGAHARA, ONIME NO KYO, OR "DEMON EYES KYO," WAS SAID TO HAVE KILLED 1000 MEN, AND FOR HIS CRIMES A ONE MILLION RYO BOUNTY HAS BEEN PLACED ON HIS HEAD. SOMEHOW, AFTER SEKIGAHARA, KYO'S SPIRIT BECAME TRAPPED INSIDE KYOSHIRO'S BODY. NOW KYOSHIRO'S SPIRIT IS TRAPPED AND KYO'S SPIRIT CONTROLS THE BODY.

YUYA SHIINA

YUYA SHIINA—A BOUNTY HUNTRESS WHO SAYS SHE'S THE BEST ON KOKAIDO-CHU. SHE ONLY GOES AFTER THE MOST HIGH-PROFILE CRIMINALS WITH THE HIGHEST BOUNTIES. SHE IS ARMED WITH A THREE-BARRELED PISTOL AND SHE CAN THROW KNIVES WITH DEADLY ACCURACY, BUT PERHAPS HER GREATEST WEAPON IS HER FEMININE WILES. IN ADDITION TO HER BOUNTY HUNTING, SHE ALSO SEARCHES FOR A MAN WITH A SCAR WHO IS SOMEHOW CONNECTED TO HER PAST.

IZUMO NO OKUNI

IZUMO NO OKUNI—A PAID INFORMANT, THIS BEAUTIFUL BACK-STABBER IS MORE THAN SHE LETS ON. SHE KNOWS DEMON EYES KYO AND SEEMS TO HAVE HAD SOME SORT OF RELATIONSHIP WITH HIM IN THE PAST.

YUKIMURA SANADA

YUKIMURA SANADA—SON OF A WEALTHY AND POWERFUL FAMILY, SANADA WANTS THE HEAD OF IEYASU TOKUGAWA AND HOPES KYO WILL GET IT FOR HIM. HE IS FOND OF DRINK AND WOMEN, BUT WHEN THE OCCASION CALLS FOR IT, HE IS A MASTER WITH THE SWORD.

BENITORA "THE RED TIGER"

BENITORA, THE "RED TIGER"—DON'T LET HIS KITTEN-LIKE EXTERIOR FOOL YOU. THIS TIGER'S TRUE STRIPES ARE OF A MUCH MORE SAVAGE NATURE. BENITORA'S WEAPON OF CHOICE IS THE CROSS HAND SPEAR, A COLLAPSIBLE POLE WITH A THREE-BLADED CROSS AT THE END. HE SPEAKS IN KANSAI DIALECT AND IS A SHAMELESS FLIRT.

OBAASAN

"OBAASAN"—THIS NAMELESS OLD WOMAN IS THE ONLY REMAINING RESIDENT OF THE MOUNTAIN WHICH GENMA KIDOU IS TRYING TO TAKE. THE BEAUTIFUL SAKURA TREE ON HER MOUNTAIN IS A REMINDER OF HER LOST LOVE AND SHE REFUSES TO ABANDON IT. YUYA (AND KYOSHIRO BY PROXY) HAS VOLUNTEERED TO BE HER BODYGUARD.

Four years after the bloody Battle of Sekigahara, the paths of the mysterious medicine peddler, **Kyoshiro Mibu**, and the bounty huntress, **Yuya Shiina**, happened to cross.

Yuya soon realized there was much more to her companion than meets the eye.

Two spirits trapped in one body:
The peaceful Kyoshiro... And the legendary samurai,

I THINK WE SHOULD GO THIS WAY.

The two travel west, each in pursuit of their own goal...

ONE MILLION RYO BOUNTY FOR KYO. 100 MON FOR KYOSHIRO.
I'LL USE MY FEMININE WILES TO SUBDUE HIM! THEN I'LL HAVE ALL THE MONEY I NEED TO HUNT DOWN THE MAN WITH THE SCAR.

The tables are turned when **Izumo no Okuni** whispers something to Kyoshiro, releasing Kyo's spirit permanently. Now Kyo calls the shots and Yuya follows on his terms... at least until the opportunity arises for her to collect the bounty.

They are joined by **Benitora**, formerly of the Three Colors Gang. Together they head for Edo where supposedly there is someone who can solve the problem of Kyo and Kyoshiro's curse.

On the road, they meet a drunk who seems to know Kyo.

Upon arriving in Edo, the man is revealed to be Yukimura Sanada of the Demon Clan, and he has an interesting proposition for Kyo...

KYO-SAN... DO WE HAVE A DEAL? YOU BRING ME THE SHOGUN IEYASU TOKUGAWA'S HEAD...
...AND I'LL TELL YOU WHERE KYOSHIRO HID YOUR BODY.

WHAT ?!
....
BUT YOU DON'T HAVE MUCH CHOICE, DO YOU? UNLESS YOU DO ME THIS FAVOR, THE IGA NINJAS WILL NEVER STOP HUNTING YOU.

SAMURAI DEEPER
KYO

BOUND FOREVER, RIGHT?

WHAT LUCK!
I COME FOR YUKIMURA AND FIND DEMON EYES KYO?!
DEMON EYES KYO, YOUR DAYS ARE NUMBERED. I, THE SPIDER WOMAN MAHIRO...
...WILL FINALLY HAVE MY REVENGE!

SAMURAI DEEPER
KYO
CHAPTER 24
SPIDER WOMAN

IF YOU WIN THE CHAMPIONSHIP, IEYASU WILL GIVE YOU THE PRIZE PERSONALLY.
THAT'S THE ONLY CHANCE YOU HAVE.
YOU MUST KILL HIM WITHOUT HESITATION.
CAN YOU DO IT?
...

I DON'T KNOW.
Why don't you do it?

WHY?

IF YOU WANT TO KNOW WHERE YOUR BODY IS HIDDEN, YOU SHOULD STOP BEING SO DIFFICULT!
I'VE HEARD ENOUGH.

IF YOU THINK YOU CAN PLAY ME, YOU'RE DUMBER THAN I THOUGHT.
COVER YOUR OWN ASS. STOP WORRYING ABOUT MINE.

......
HUH?

YOU'RE SO CALM AND COLLECTED. YOU'RE A LEGEND, AND YOU RISE HEAD AND SHOULDERS ABOVE COMMON MEN!
WHAT?

YOU'RE SO HOLY, YOU WALK ALONE IN HEAVEN AND ON EARTH.
I could fall in love.
YOU DON'T NEED ANYONE.

RIGHT?

BUT THEN, WHAT HAPPENS AFTER 10 MINUTES, KYO-SAN?

WHAT? WHAT?

10 MINUTES?

AFTER ALL, YOU ARE ONLY BORROWING KYOSHIRO'S BODY. YOU CAN'T CONTROL IT FOREVER, ESPECIALLY UNDER DURESS.
THE CONCENTRATION REQUIRED DURING A SUDDEN-DEATH BATTLE IS NEARLY UNFATHOMABLE. IF THE BATTLE RAGES ON FOR TOO LONG, YOU MIGHT LOSE THE BALANCE BETWEEN YOUR SOUL AND THAT BODY.
YOU COULD EASILY SWITCH BACK TO KYOSHIRO. OR, EVEN WORSE, *YOUR SOUL COULD BE LOST FOREVER*.
THAT'S WHY THERE WILL BE A *10 MINUTE TIME LIMIT*. IT'S RATHER INCONVENIENT, BUT I BET YOU WANT TO GET YOUR BODY BACK PRETTY BADLY.
AM I WRONG?
WHO TOLD YOU ALL THAT?
I'M... NOT... TELLING...
IS HE TELLING THE TRUTH?
WHAT DOES IT MATTER?
EVEN IF I ONLY HAVE 10 MINUTES...
...IT'S MORE THAN ENOUGH TIME TO KILL EVERYONE I NEED.
IF YOU WANT IEYASU DEAD, FIND ANOTHER MONKEY.
HEY! YOU CAN'T LEAVE NOW! HEY, BENITORA, YOU'RE THE RED TIGER, SO POUNCE! GET UP!
GET UP, DAMN YOU!
....

HEY! KYO!
HEY! WAIT!
WHAT IS IT, CHATTERBOX?
WHAT HAPPENED TO THE RED TIGER?
I LEFT HIM ON THE FLOOR!
BUT THE WAY YOU TREATED YUKIMURA ...
SO STRONG ...
I REALLY SAW YOU IN A NEW LIGHT!

WE JUST NEED TO WATCH THE TIME AND THERE WON'T BE ANY PROBLEMS.
BUT I KNOW SOMETHING WE CAN DO FOR MORE THAN 10 MINUTES ...
HUH?
I'M ASKING YOU...
...TO TAKE ME...

TAKE ME NOW. YOU CAN HAVE MY BODY...
...
SCUTTY
SCUTTY
OH, KYO...

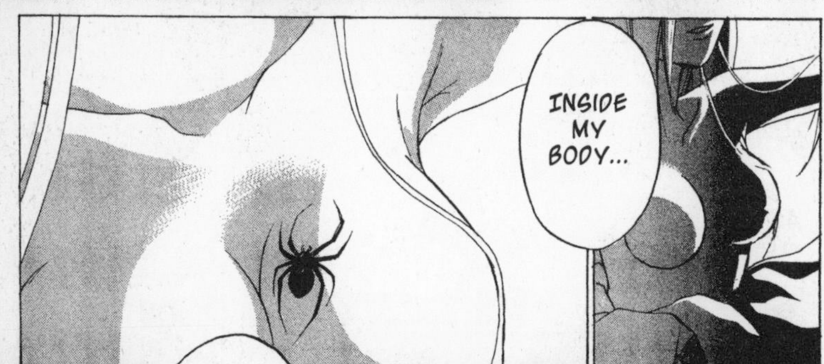
INSIDE MY BODY...

...YOU'LL FIND THE HEAVEN YOU DESIRE.

!!

LOOK, WOMAN, I DON'T KNOW WHO YOU ARE...

...BUT YOU'RE DOING A HORRIBLE IMPERSON-ATION OF YUYA.
Crunch!

......
SURE, YOU HAVE THE LOOK DOWN, BUT YUYA KNOWS THAT SHE CAN'T JUST DAB ON SOME PERFUME AND SEDUCE ME...

...BECAUSE, FRANKLY, SHE'S NOT THAT ATTRACTIVE.
HEY! KYOO OOO!
COME BACK HERE!
Yaaa awn!

LISTEN, YOU! YOU CAN'T LEAVE MY SIDE WITHOUT TELLING ME!
You're an important bounty!
YOU CAN'T JUST WALK OUT OF THE TEA HOUSE!
WHAT?
KYAAAA! SHE-SHE LOOKS JUST LIKE ME!
ばっ

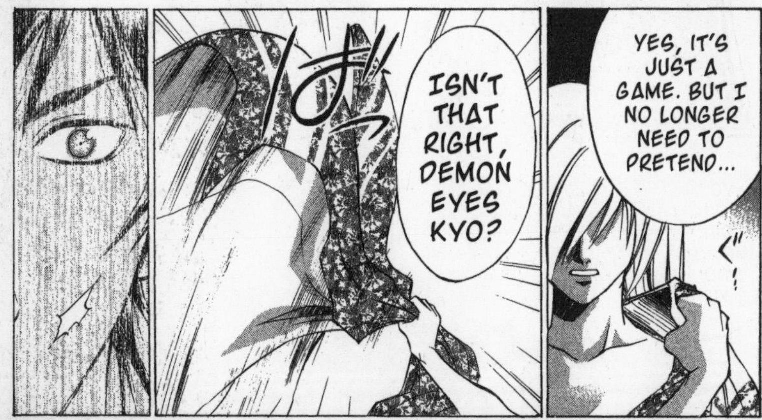
YES, IT'S JUST A GAME. BUT I NO LONGER NEED TO PRETEND...
ぐ
ISN'T THAT RIGHT, DEMON EYES KYO?

YOU ARE...

MAHIRO... MAHIRO, ISN'T IT?
YOU SURPRISE ME, KYO.
I WAS CERTAIN YOU WOULD HAVE FORGOTTEN.

...
I'VE HUNTED YOU FOR FOUR YEARS...
YOU CAN FORGET ABOUT HUNTING IEYASU. HIS HEAD WILL REMAIN INTACT.
BY THE SAME TOKEN, I CAN'T HAVE THE IGA NINJAS HUNTING YOU. YOU'RE ALL MINE.
I'M GOING TO PUT YOU TO SLEEP FOREVER.
I CAME BACK FROM THE EDGE OF HELL TO DO JUST THAT.
I'VE HELD A NASTY GRUDGE FOR A LONG TIME.
AND IT'S TIME FOR ME TO PAY YOU BACK!
YOU'LL SUFFER FOR THE HUMILIATION THAT MY SISTER ENDURED AND FOR THE PAIN THAT TORMENTED BOTH ARMS!!
AND I'M NOT GONNA KILL YOU RIGHT AWAY. OH, NO! YOU'LL WRITHE IN AGONY FIRST!
AT THE TOURNAMENT, IN FIVE DAYS...
THAT IS WHERE ...

...YOU SHALL AT LONG LAST DIE!

GYAAA!
WHAT ARE THEY ?!
BLACK WIDOWS!
ONE BITE AND WE'RE DONE!
YUYA-HAN!! DON'T LET THEM TOUCH YOU!
THAT'S IMPOSSIBLE. THERE ARE TOO MANY...
YAAAAAA!

I DON'T BELIEVE IT!
WHY DID HE SAVE US?
WHAT AM I THINKING?!
HE'S JUST A COLD-BLOODED KILLER! A VICIOUS MURDERER!
But maybe that's not entirely true.
HEY! THAT NINJA WOMAN TOOK OFF IN A HUFF.
WHAT?!
!?
I NEVER EVEN SAW HER LEAVE!
KYO... WHO WAS SHE?
......

I CAN'T BELIEVE ...
...SHE'S STILL ALIVE.

HUH?
WHAT HAPPENED ...
...BETWEEN YOU AND THAT WOMAN?

SEE. I TOLD YOU.

YUKI-MURA!
THE ASSASSINS ARE ALREADY OUT FOR YOUR BLOOD, KYO.
I'm glad she didn't come to my place.

SO, KYO-SAN...HAVE YOU HAD A CHANGE OF HEART?
...
YUKIMURA DOESN'T REALIZE IT'S HOPELESS ONCE KYO MAKES UP HIS MIND...
I'LL DO IT.
WHAT?!
I'LL FIGHT IN THE TOURNAMENT.
I'LL BRING YOU IEYASU'S HEAD.

After arriving in Edo, Kyo contemplates a deal offered by the eccentric Yukimura. In exchange for killing Ieyasu at a tournament, Yukimura will give Kyo the one thing he desires most.

But ***Mahiro****, a mysterious woman who has an army of trained spiders has appeared from Kyo's past, vowing revenge on Kyo for killing her sister four years before.*

And Kyo suddenly accepted Yukimura's offer!

What is the real meaning behind Kyo's change of heart?

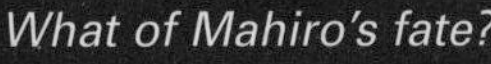

What of Mahiro's fate?

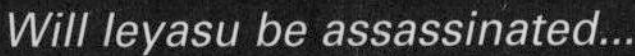

Will Ieyasu be assassinated...

...by Kyo at the tournament?

Finally, the battle has come!

SAMURAI DEEPER KYO

THIS...
SAMURAI DEEPER KYO
CHAPTER 25
BATTLE BEFORE THE SHOGUN
...IS WHERE THE TOURNAMENT SHALL BE HELD!
WOW. IT'S HUGE.
IMPRES-SIVE.
......

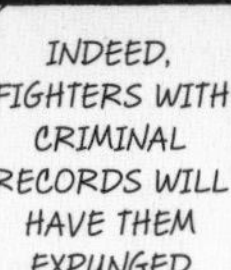

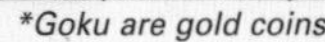

THE TOURNAMENT IS HELD...
...IN HONOR OF THE "GREAT" IEYASU'S BIRTHDAY, SINCE HE LOVES MARTIAL ARTS. FIGHTERS FROM THROUGHOUT JAPAN WILL COME TO COMPETE FOR PRIDE AND HONOR.
THE WINNER WILL RECEIVE 10,000 RYO AND 1,000 GOKU*. IT IS ASSURED THAT THE MOST FEARSOME FIGHTERS WILL ATTEND.
INDEED, FIGHTERS WITH CRIMINAL RECORDS WILL HAVE THEM EXPUNGED IF THEY ARE VICTORIOUS.
SINCE THE LOWEST RUNGS OF SOCIETY WILL BE THERE, I AM SURE NO ONE WILL BAT A LASH IF DEMON EYES KYO MAKES AN APPEARANCE.
I WANT YOU TO WIN THE TOURNAMENT...
...THEN IT'S OFF WITH IEYASU'S HEAD!
Are you ready to make it roll?
Of course, you won't get the prize money.
BUT I'M SURE YOU'D RATHER HAVE YOUR BODY.
...
I'LL BE CLOSE BY, WATCHING. GOOD LUCK.

*Goku are gold coins.

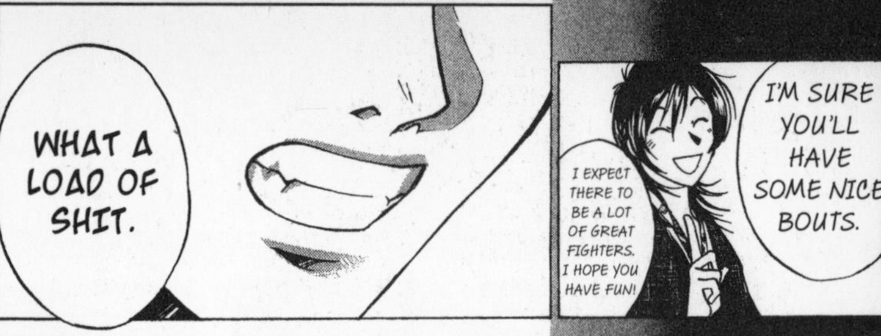

I'M SURE YOU'LL HAVE SOME NICE BOUTS.
I EXPECT THERE TO BE A LOT OF GREAT FIGHTERS. I HOPE YOU HAVE FUN!
WHAT A LOAD OF SHIT.

SO MANY FIGHTERS!

Oh, I know that guy. He's a dirty jerk!

Championship Arena

Preliminary Arena

They are here.

WHAT ?

WHAT THE...

Why you...

WHAT'D YOU SAY?

WHERE'RE YOUR SMART-ASS COMMENTS NOW?
NOT SO BRAVE WHEN A BIG FISH COMES AROUND, HUH?
I'VE KILLED OVER 100 PEOPLE...
MOST OF THEM, BECAUSE I DIDN'T LIKE HOW THEY LOOKED.
I COULD SNAP A TWIG LIKE YOU IN HALF WITH MY TEETH!
YES, YOU COULD KILL SOMEONE WITH YOUR MOUTH...

...SINCE IT REEKS LIKE THE CRAP YOU SPEAK.
KYAAAAA!

STOP!
ANY TROUBLE-MAKERS WILL BE BANNED FROM THE TOURNA-MENT!

GR RR...
....

NOW PAY ATTEN-TION!

HERE ARE THE RULES FOR ROUND ONE!

THIS TOURNAMENT IS HELD IN HONOR OF THE GREAT IEYASU-SAMA'S BIRTHDAY. THE WINNER WILL BE ALLOWED TO MEET HIS HONOR! IEYASU-SAMA HIMSELF WILL AWARD THE GRAND PRIZE.

THE LOSER OF EACH BOUT IS THE FIRST MAN TO YIELD OR BE KNOCKED UNCONSCIOUS BY THE BOKUTO*.

IF YOU KILL YOUR OPPONENT, YOU WILL FORFEIT THE MATCH! YOU WILL BE DIVIDED INTO EIGHT MATCHES AT A TIME, TWO COMBATANTS PER MATCH. THERE IS NO TIME LIMIT.

*Bokuto is a wooden sword.

WHAT A PAIN.
...

NO TIME LIMIT?
THAT MIGHT CAUSE TROUBLE FOR KYO.
AHH... DON'T WORRY ABOUT IT.
SEE ...

5 MINUTES, 10, 20...THE WOLF WILL ALWAYS BEAT THE SHEEP.

SO THE TOURNA-MENT BEGINS ...
AND KYO HAS COME TO FIGHT.

I WILL NEVER FORGET WHAT YOU HAVE DONE TO ME...
NEVER.
IT'S BEEN 4 YEARS ...

I HOPE YOU ARE WATCHING, SISTER...
WATCHING ME CLAIM VENGEANCE IN YOUR NAME.

THE FIRST MATCH SHALL BE KINZABURO-DONO VERSUS KYO-DONO!
HEH-HEH-HEH... SHALL WE MAKE A PROMISE TO FINISH WHAT WE'VE STARTED?
NO KILLING?! I DON'T CARE. I'VE ALREADY DECIDED TO KILL YOU.
IF YOU DON'T LIKE IT, CRY TO THE FATES, BECAUSE TODAY YOU ARE DESTINED TO DIE.
ギ
ばっ

MAHIRO...
...

WHAT?! YOU DARE TURN YOUR BACK ON ME?!
YOU WISH FOR A QUICK DEATH, THEN?
KYO! WATCH OUT!
HAHA HAHA! TOO LATE, GIRL!
WHAT?! HOW'D HE-
HEY, REF!
Y... YES?
CAN I FIGHT THE WHOLE GROUP AT THE SAME TIME?
I'll kill them all.

WHAT?!

HUH?!

ISN'T THAT A LITTLE DANGER-OUS?
MAYBE...
TO KILL THAT MANY PEOPLE... WITHOUT HIS TRUE BODY...
EVEN KYO-HAN MAY FIND THAT DIFFICULT.

HEY, YOU! WHAT'RE YOU THINKING?

TOO LATE FOR REGRETS NOW!

I DON'T LIVE WITH REGRET, FOOLS.

What are you waiting for?!

HERE, PUNK! YOU HAVE YOUR WISH!

HEY! KYO!

HEY, YOU!

KILLING IS FOR-BIDDEN!

DON'T WORRY ABOUT IT.

WHAT ?!

Yaa!

I DIDN'T KILL ANYONE.

GO CHECK IF YOU WANT.
THEY'RE ALIVE.
Or better said, half-dead.

THE WINNER OF ROUND ONE: KYO-DONO!
やぁぁぁ…
WHAT DID HE DO?
ATTACK OF THE THREE FIRES. ALL OF THEIR ORGANS BURN LIKE FIRE...
IT WAS FIVE.
WHAT ?!

THEIR ORGANS HAD FIVE FIRES EACH.

ひょんっ

WHO... WHO ARE YOU?

WHAT ?

What a beautiful chick!

IT'S ME. ME! CAN'T YOU TELL?

YUKI-MURA, WHAT ARE YOU UP TO NOW?

I'M TIRED OF YOUR GAMES!
WHAT ?!
WHY ARE YOU DRESSED LIKE A GIRL ?!
CONSIDER IT A DISGUISE. I WANTED TO FIGHT IN THE TOURNAMENT.
Don't I look fabulous?
HAHAHA! BUT WE COULD HAVE SO MUCH FUN PLAYING TOGETHER, KYO-SAN.
DIDN'T I TELL YOU I'D BE CLOSE BY?
AND ...
...SAKUYA-SAN WANTED ME TO.

WHAT?!
OKAY! I'LL SEE YOU LATER!
I'm in shock.
......
....
WHAT?! THAT VILLAIN SNUCK IN?
IS IT TRUE, HANZO?

OUR NINJAS HAVE FAILED. YOUR LIFE IS AT RISK. WE MUST POSTPONE THE TOURNAMENT.

DON'T WORRY, HANZO. EVERYTHING WILL GO AS PLANNED.

WHAT?

WITHOUT A LITTLE INTRIGUE, OUR LIVES...

...WOULD BE VERY DULL.

HEY ...

ザワ...

IT CAN'T BE...

WHAT'S THAT NOISE?

I DON'T KNOW ...

....

IS IT...
HOW LONG WAS JAPAN SPLIT BY CIVIL WAR BEFORE THE BATTLE OF SEKIGAHARA?
HERE HE IS, THE MAN WHOSE FAMILY UNIFIED THE LAND AND BROUGHT PEACE.
A PEACE THAT ONLY THE RICH CAN BUY WITH THEIR BLOOD MONEY.
TOKUGAWA...
IEYASU.

SAMURAI DEEPER
KYO
THE WINNER FROM GROUP 3...
THE RED TIGER! BENI-TORA!
YAAAA!
YOU DID IT! AND I SEE YOU'RE WORTH 50 RYO OF BOUNTY!
IT WAS A PIECE OF CAKE!
きゃっ
WHY ARE YOU FIGHTING IN THE TOURNA-MENT?
はっ
WELL... SORRY...BUT I JUST WANT TO TEST MY SKILLS AGAINST STRONG SAMURAI.
SO I DECIDED TO ENTER.
THE WINNER OF THIS TOURNA-MENT WILL BECOME RICH AND FAMOUS!
AND THEN I CAN TELL YUYA-HAN MY TRUE FEELINGS!
IF IT WEREN'T FOR HIS BOUNTY, HE'D BE USELESS.
ALL WINNERS OF ROUND ONE, PLEASE PROCEED TO THE INNER SHINTO SHRINE.

WOW. THEY ALL LOOK SO TOUGH.
THEY ARE.
THEY ALL LOOK LIKE CROOKS AND ASSASSINS, IF YOU ASK ME.
I'M EAGER TO SEE WHO'LL WIN!
YEAH.
I'll be the one who laughs last.
BENI-TORA...
YES?
DO YOU KNOW EVERYONE'S IDENTITY?
...
YOU MEAN WHERE THEY ARE FROM?

SAMURAI DEEPER
KYO
CHAPTER 25: AMBITION IN THE MOONLIGHT
BUT HOW DOES...
...MAHIRO FIT INTO ALL OF THIS?
KYO-HAN.
YUKI-MURA-HAN.
I'M RIGHT SO FAR...
Yes.
AND THE REST OF THEM...
THOSE THREE...

STRONG ARM SHICHIRO UEMON. REAPER KORESTU. THE KILLER MOTONAGA SAEKI.
THEY'VE CHANGED THEIR NAMES, BUT THERE'S STILL A BOUNTY ON EACH HEAD.
They're not as good as me, though.
STRONG ARM SHICHIRO UEMON. HIS NAME REVEALS HIS WEAPON-BRUTE STRENGTH.
THERE'S A RUMOR HE EATS ANYONE HE KILLS. WEIRD GUY.
...
KORESTU IS AMBIDEXTROUS.
HE HAS A STRANGE FETISH FOR KILLING WOMEN. THEY SAY HE ONCE CLOGGED A TOWN'S RIVER WITH THE BODIES OF PROSTITUTES.
Ummm mum um...
Ummm umum
MOTONAGA SAEKI. HIS WEAPON IS THE SWORD.
HE IS A RONIN WHO SELLS HIS BLADE TO THE HIGHEST BIDDER.
WOW. THEY'RE ALL TERRIBLE...
I CAN DO SOME BOUNTY HUNTING HERE.
BUT IF YOU ASK ME, THEY'LL BE EASY TO BEAT.
THE ONE I'D WORRY ABOUT IS...

...THAT MAN. SHIGEKATA TOGO. HE GRADUATED FROM THE JIGEN SCHOOL.

WHAT'S HE LIKE?
I'M NOT SURE. I KNOW HE'S TRAINING TO BE A SWORD INSTRUCTOR IN THE SATSUMA FEUDAL CLAN.

THE SATSUMA FEUDAL CLAN ENCOURAGES A NATIONAL ISOLATIONIST POLICY, AND THE JIGEN SCHOOL IS QUITE MYSTERIOUS ...
BUT, I'VE HEARD THAT A SAMURAI SKILLED WITH THE TACHI* CAN SPLIT A MAN IN HALF.

*A tachi is a type of long sword.

I'D LOVE TO SEE THAT!
I CAN'T WAIT TO SEE HIM IN ACTION.

STRONG. THEY ARE ALL STRONG...
OH... THERE'S ONE MORE PERSON ...
...

HMMM. I DON'T KNOW WHO THAT IS...
WHAT ?!

THAT MAN IN THE WILD WIG...HE WEARS A **BEAST MASK**...

jingle jingle

I KNOW NOTHING OF HIM. HE HIDES BEHIND A MASK.
I HAVEN'T HEARD A WORD...

HE'S ADVANCED THIS FAR...
...BUT HE HASN'T HAD A SINGLE MATCH.

WHAT?

EACH TIME HE STEPPED INTO THE RING...
...HIS OPPONENT FAILED TO SHOW UP.

WHY?
DUNNO. BUT IT SOUNDS SUS-PICIOUS TO ME.

...
BUT, KYO-HAN...

...IF THERE IS ONE PERSON YOU'RE SEARCHING FOR, IT'S PROBABLY THAT GUY.

THE FINAL MATCHES WILL BE HELD TOMORROW MORNING...
HERE, BEFORE THE MAIN SHINTO SHRINE.

BANG!
ATTACK!
TAKE THIS! SHOKIN KOMACHI ATTACK!
...

FOG...

す…
ヌク…
ぉっ

!?
HOW?! WE FILLED THE ROOM WITH SLEEPING INCENSE!
YOU... YOU'RE NOT MAHIRO!
ANY FOOL WHO WOULD RAISE A SWORD TO ME IS A DEAD FOOL...
GUH!
DO YOU UNDER-STAND ?!

KYO-SAN! WAIT!
PLEASE FORGIVE ME, BUT...
...HE WORKS FOR ME.

......

THIS MAN WAS MERELY TESTING YOUR SKILLS.
HE WAS BEING FAITHFUL TO HIS MASTER. PLEASE FORGIVE HIM FOR MY SAKE...

THANK YOU, KYO-SAN...
SAIZO.
YES.

I ALWAYS BELIEVED YOU WERE INTELLIGENT, YUKIMURA. YET, YOU SEND YOUR MEN...
...TO SHAMELESSLY KILL ME IN THE NIGHT?
SORRY. I JUST WANTED TO SEE-
...
YUKIMURA...

WHY DO YOU WANT TO KILL IEYASU?

......

LONG AGO, THERE WAS A MAN NAMED NOBUSHIGE TOYOTOMI.

HE WAS FROM A WELL-KNOWN CLAN. IN FACT, A CITY WAS GIVEN THE TOYOTOMI NAME DUE TO HIS DISTINGUISHED CONTRIBUTIONS. THEY WERE ALLIES OF THE SHOGUN TOYOTOMI HEDEYOSHI. AT THE BATTLE OF SEKIGAHARA...
...NOBUSHIGE CAST HIS LOT WITH HEDEYOSHI AGAINST TOKUGAWA.
THE HEDEYOSHI FORCES WERE CRUSHED. NOBUSHIGE AND HIS FAMILY FLED TO KUDO MOUNTAIN IN KISHU.
IN TIME, THEY EVEN GREW TO LIKE IT THERE.
BUT ALWAYS, DEEP IN HIS HEART, HE BURNED WITH HATRED FOR TOKUGAWA. HE HAD SAID...

"I WOULD RATHER...

...SEE IEYASU'S HEAD ROLL...

...THAN RULE THE WHOLE OF THIS LAND."

BUT THE TRUTH IS...
...THAT MAN NEVER EXPECTED HEDEYOSHI'S FORCES TO WIN.
THEN WHY DID HE SACRIFICE SO MUCH FOR HEDEYOSHI?

MAYBE... MAYBE HE JUST LIKED HIM.

YES, HEDEYOSHI IS SOMEWHAT UNSOPHISTI-CATED...
...BUT HE HAS SUCH A FRIENDLY AND INNOCENT FACE.
PEOPLE CAN'T HELP BUT LIKE HIM SO MUCH.

YUKIMURA
...

BY THE WAY, KYO-SAN!
DO YOU REALLY KNOW WHY I ASKED YOU TO KILL IEYASU?
I MEET YOU AT A TEAHOUSE AND THEN JUST ASK YOU FOR SUCH A BURDENSOME FAVOR? DIDN'T THAT SEEM ODD TO YOU?
...
THE TRUTH IS...

...WE HAVE MET BEFORE.
AT SEKIGAHARA.

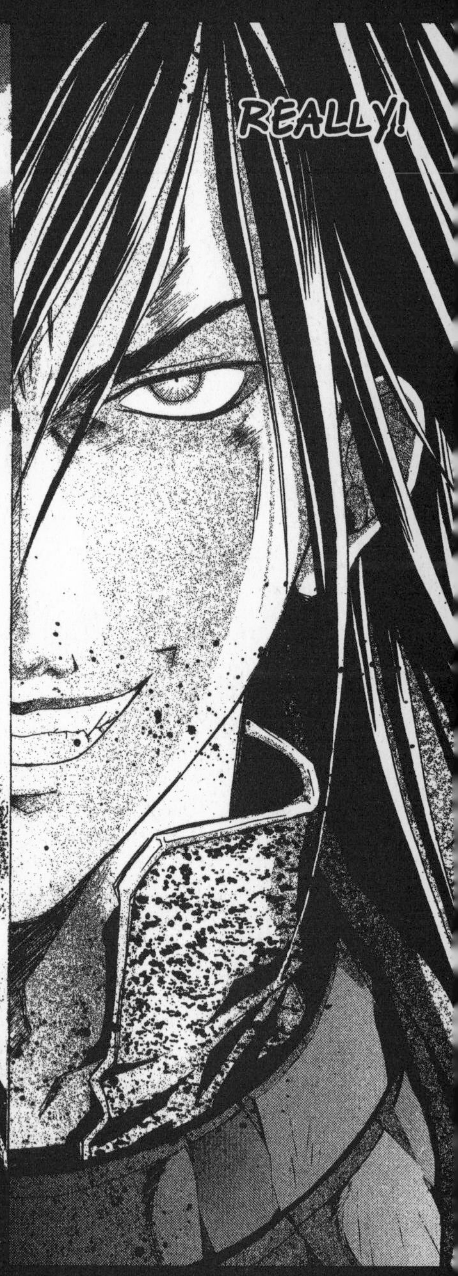

ON THE BATTLEFIELD, AMIDST THE DARKNESS AND THE DEATH...

...YOU WALKED ALONE IN BLOODY ROBES.

LOOKING FOR SURVIVORS.

WITH BEAUTIFUL... BEAUTIFUL... GLOWING RED EYES.

AT THAT TIME, I THOUGHT...
"HE'S NOT HUMAN."
....
I KNEW YOU COULD BEAT TOKUGAWA... AND HIS ENTIRE LEGION.

YOU SHOULDN'T SAY SUCH THINGS.
HAHAHA! YOU'RE PROBABLY RIGHT.
Maybe I should keep a tighter lip.
I'VE HAD A FEW MISUNDERSTANDINGS ...
....

Don't lose your courage!

...WITH THAT GIRL, MAHIRO.
ISN'T SHE THE REAL REASON YOU DECIDED TO TAKE MY OFFER?
SUCH A TRAGEDY.

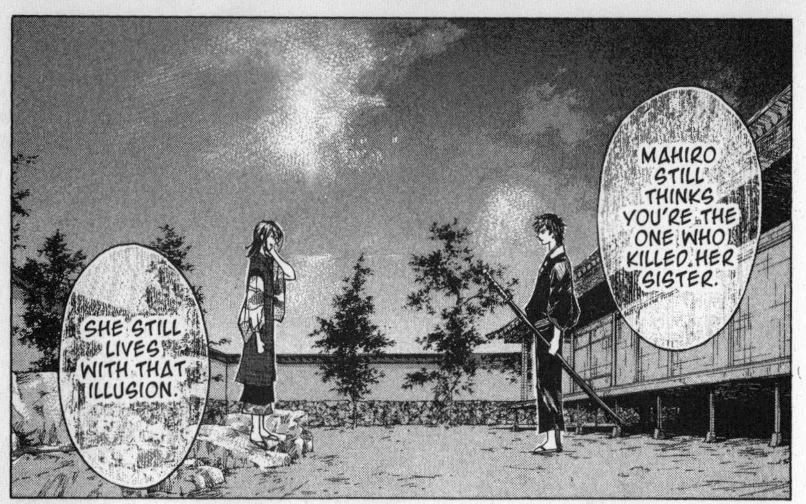

MAHIRO STILL THINKS YOU'RE THE ONE WHO KILLED HER SISTER.
SHE STILL LIVES WITH THAT ILLUSION.

BECAUSE OF THAT BELIEF, SHE HAS LOWERED HERSELF TO BECOMING A DISHONOR-ABLE NINJA...
...AND NOW SHE'S TRYING TO KILL THE MAN SHE LOVED.
YOU...

TO CLEAR YOUR NAME, YOU'VE DECIDED TO FIGHT IN THE TOURNAMENT?!
AH HA HA
EASY... TOO EASY!
WHO WOULD THINK THAT THE DREADED KYO-SAN...
...WOULD HAVE SUCH A TENDER HEART?

BUT THEN, PERHAPS THAT IS WHY I LIKE YOU.

WHO TOLD YOU THESE THINGS?

SHALL I TELL YOU?

TELL YOU HOW I KNOW SO MUCH ABOUT YOU?
WELL...
I ASKED KYOSHIRO TO TELL ME ABOUT YOU...
...WHEN WE HID YOUR BODY TOGETHER.

WHAT?!
OH? DIDN'T YOU HEAR ME?
I SAID ...
...I ASKED KYOSHIRO TO TELL ME ABOUT YOU...
...WHEN WE HID YOUR BODY TOGETHER.
SAMURAI DEEPER KYO
CHAPTER 27
THE NIGHT BEFORE

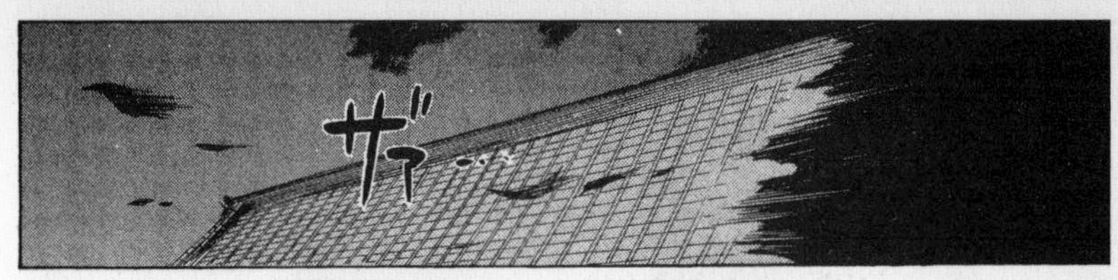

I DON'T- YOU AND KYOSHIRO ARE WORKING TOGETHER?
I WOULDN'T SAY "WORKING." HE WAS IN TROUBLE AND I JUST GAVE HIM A LITTLE NUDGE.

BUT I DIDN'T REALIZE HOW MUCH IT COULD HELP ME NOW!

DON'T BE STUPID!

HUH?

YOU'RE NOT THE KIND OF PERSON TO JUST "HELP" SOMEONE. WHAT WAS IN IT FOR YOU?

AND HOW THE HELL DO YOU KNOW ABOUT MAHIRO?

WHAT'S YOUR REAL RELATIONSHIP WITH KYOSHIRO?

...

I CAN'T TELL YOU. IT'S A SECRET BETWEEN KYOSHIRO-SAN AND MYSELF.

BESIDES...

クス

SOME THINGS ARE BETTER LEFT UNKNOWN.
クス…
AND THERE'S JUST NO REASON TO TELL YOU.

ザァ…
I WILL ONLY ASK YOU ONE MORE TIME...
スル…
NOPE.

サァァ

IT WOULD BE A WASTE.

HUH?

TO KILL ALL OF THEM AT ONCE.

COME OUT! IT'S A WASTE OF TIME TO TRY HIDING...

COME AND LET ME SEE...

...THE LEGENDARY WARRIOR HEROES OF SANADA!

SANADA'S TEN-WARRIOR HEROES.
THEY WORK LIKE THE HANDS AND LEGS OF YUKIMURA SANADA, PROTECTING HIS "DEMON" CLAN.
IT IS SAID THAT EACH HAS THE STRENGTH OF 1,000 SAMURAI.

I WON'T LET THEM FIGHT YOU.
THEIR ANGER SPEAKS DIFFERENTLY.
I can sense it.

EVERYONE, STAND DOWN!

FOR THE SAKE OF YOUR FAITHFUL DOGS, I WILL LET YOU GO THIS TIME.
I'd hate to humiliate them in front of their master.

ARE YOU GOING TO BACK OUT?
TO WHOM ARE YOU SPEAKING... YUKIMURA?

YUKIMURA-SAMA...

...IT PAINS ME TO SIT IDLE AND LISTEN TO HIM SPEAK TO YOU IN SUCH A RUDE MANNER!
PLEASE GIVE US THE ORDER. THE TEN OF US CAN SURELY KILL HIM!

YUKIMURA-SAMA! PLEASE!
DOES HE FRIGHTEN YOU, SAIZO?
....
YUKIMURA-SAMA! I...I... YES...

I FEAR THE MAN, BUT NOT DEATH! I WOULD GIVE MY LIFE TO DEFEND YOU!
AS WOULD ALL OF US!
SAIZO ...

THERE IS NO SHAME IN FEARING KYO.
IN FACT, I WOULD THINK YOU A FOOL IF YOU DID NOT. YOU WILL FIND COURAGE IN THAT TRUTH.

TERRIFYING. THAT MAN IS TERRIFYING.
BUT I CANNOT HELP BUT TO CRAVE A FIGHT WITH HIM.
ONCE MORE, I TOO...
...CAN BE STRONG, SAIZO.

YUKIMURA-SAMA ...
HE IS SERIOUS ...
EVEN THOUGH YOU WERE NOT AT FULL STRENGTH AT SEKIGAHARA, IEYASU FEARED YOU!
THE SLEEPING DRAGON AWAKENS AT LAST!
I...
I'M MORE FRIGHTENED OF YOU, YUKIMURA-SAMA...

THOSE BASTARD ASSASSINS THAT HATTORI HANZO WAS TALKING ABOUT... THE RUMORS SEEM TO BE TRUE- THEY ARE HIDING.
I...
I AGREE WITH HANZO-DONO, MY LORD. WE ASK THAT YOU RECONSIDER. PLEASE STOP THE FINAL MATCH AND SAVE YOURSELF!
HOW OLD DID YOU TURN THIS YEAR?
I... I'M THIRTY-EIGHT.
I SEE ...
THIS YEAR, I HAVE REACHED SIXTY-THREE.
SOON, IT SHALL BE TIME FOR ME TO GET READY.
GET READY?

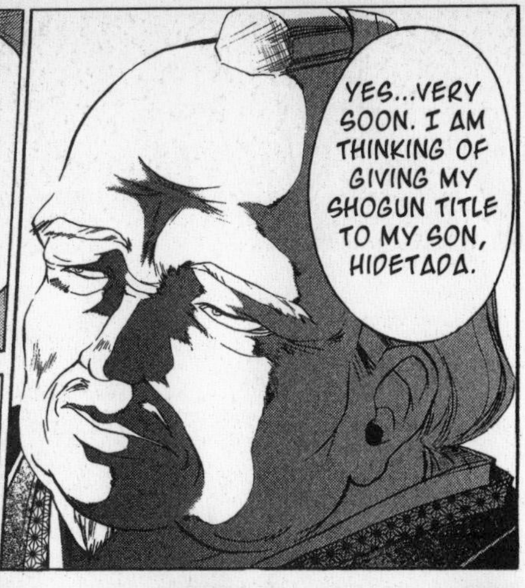
YES...VERY SOON. I AM THINKING OF GIVING MY SHOGUN TITLE TO MY SON, HIDETADA.

BUT THE BOY IS NOT A SAMURAI BORN. HE IS NOT EVEN THE EQUAL OF NOBUYASU OR HEDEYASU.
THE TOKUGAWA GOVERNMENT IS STILL WEAK, AND I HAVE BECOME OLD. I NEED TO GIVE BOTH EVERY ADVANTAGE I CAN.

AND SO... THIS TOURNAMENT?
THAT'S RIGHT.

WHO COMES TO FIGHT? SCUM AND JUNKIES. ASSASSINS AND CRIMINALS. LET THE THREATS TO THE TOKUGAWA DYNASTY WEED THEMSELVES OUT.
THE WINNERS MOVE TO THE NEXT ROUND. AS FOR THE LOSERS? ONLY THE SILENCE OF THE GRAVE.
CONSIDER IT...A FINAL HOUSE CLEANING.
YES...

STRONG ARM SHICHIRO UEMON. REAPER KORESTU. KILLER MOTONAGA SAEKI...
ARE ALL ASSASSINS WITH TIES TO MORI, UESUGI AND DATE.

HOWEVER, WE ARE UNSURE OF THE OTHER THREE'S POLITICAL MOTIVATIONS.
TOGO SHIGEKATA, BENITORA AND KYO.
HMM MM...

KYO...

WHAT IS IT, MY LORD?
THE EYES...
THE DEEP-SET, DEMONIC EYES...
I FEEL LIKE I'VE MET HIM SOMEWHERE ...
MY LORD ...
NO MATTER.
JUST ANOTHER CRIMINAL COME TO FIGHT, I'M SURE.
....
NOBUSHIGE SAEMON-NOSUKE TOYOTOMI.
OH, YOU MEAN, YUKIMURA SANADA...
HE'S REALIZED THAT I WON'T CONCEDE THE SHOGUNATE TO THE TOYOTOMI FAMILY. YUKIMURA IS A GREAT SAMURAI BUT...
...IT WOULD SEEM YUKIMURA HAS FORGOTTEN HIS BROTHER'S BEGGING ME TO SPARE HIS AND HIS FATHER MASAYUKI'S LIFE.
WHAT A FOOLISH MAN TO FORGET ABOUT MY MERCY.
....

NO MATTER HOW MUCH SCUM FLOATS TO THE TOP, THEY SHALL NOT TAINT THE TOKUGAWA SHOGUNATE.
YES...
Tweet!
I BUILT THIS EMPIRE ON THE BACKS OF MY WIFE AND CHILDREN.
Tweet!
MY FAMILY'S SACRIFICE SHALL NOT BE IN VAIN.
Tweet!
Tweet!
IF YOU ARE NOT TOKUGAWA, YOU ARE NOT HUMAN!
TWEET!!
...
SO MUCH HANGS IN THE BALANCE. SO MUCH DEPENDS ON...YOU.
I PLACE MUCH UPON YOUR LOYALTY.
jingle
I UNDERSTAND ...

I WONDER WHAT HAPPENED.
ちゃぷ…
かっぽ〜ん
WE WERE HAVING THE PILLOW FIGHT, AND THEN I WAS ASLEEP!
HOT!
WHEN I WOKE UP, EVERYONE WAS GONE!
Except Beni-tora, who just snored!
EVERYONE HAS THEIR OWN AGENDA ...
I'M SICK OF IT!
...
MAYBE KYO WENT TO LOOK FOR MAHIRO.
SHE WAS VERY BEAUTI-FUL.
Her breasts were too big.
WHY DON'T YOU GROW UP A BIT?
むかぁ!
OKAY, OKAY, I HAVE SMALL BREASTS!
IT'S NOT THE SIZE! IT'S THE SHAPE!
YOUR BREASTS ARE VERY NICE.
Heheheh.
ぱしゃ
ぱしゃ
WHO... WHO'S THERE?

AND I'VE GOT JUST THE THING TO GO WITH THEM...

KYO... ARE YOU HERE? ARE YOU SLEEPING YET?

THAT'S TOO BAD...

I WAS HOPING YOU AND I...

...COULD HAVE SOME FUN!

WHAT?! HE'S NOT HERE!
TOO SLOW.
YOUR MEDIOCRITY IS ONLY MATCHED BY YOUR STUPIDITY. MAHIRO...
CHA!
AAA AAH!

WHAT?! NO SPIDER TATTOO!
SHIT!
DO YOU REALLY THINK I WOULD USE THE SAME TRICK TWICE?

YOU LOOK PATHETIC.

......

YOU'LL FIND THAT WEB...

...IS LACQUERED BY A SECRET POTION OF THE IGA NINJAS. IT MAKES WEBS STICKIER AND MAKES THEM AS STRONG AS STEEL...

ギ"

...YET AS FLEXIBLE AS AN UDON NOODLE. STRUGGLE. FIGHT. BEG.

...
YOU DROPPED YOUR GUARD, THINKING SHE WAS ME...BUT THE GIRL IS UNDER MY CONTROL.

THE SPIDER'S VENOM WEAKENS HER WILL...

...AND THE WEBS PLACE HER IN MY CONTROL ...

LIKE A PUPPET, DANCING ON STRINGS TIED TO THE WILL OF MY FINGERS.
SUCH IS THE SECRET OF THE SPIDER WOMAN'S ARACHNID SPELLS!

THE FEMALE SPIDER ...
...EATS HER MATE. SHE KILLS THE ONE SHE LOVES.

YOU'RE NOT THE ONLY ONE WHO IS STRONG, KYO.

DO YOU KNOW WHY I BECAME A SPIDER WOMAN?

MAHIRO ...

I'M SURPRISED YOU LET A WOMAN TRAVEL WITH YOU...BUT I'M GLAD...
AA AH...

...
ARE YOU READY, KYO?
...
I'VE WAITED A LONG TIME...
...TO SEE YOU DIE!

ARE YOU READY, KYO?
TASTE MY SISTER'S HUMILIATION!
N-NO! I DON'T WANT TO SHOOT!
THERE ARE STILL SO MANY THINGS TO LEARN FROM THIS STUPID-
...
MY BODY!
LOOK INTO THE EYES OF DEATH, KYO!
I CAN'T CONTROL MY BODY!
SAMURAI DEEPER KYO
CHAPTER 28 THE DEMON'S MEMORIES

chuuhk

ぎぎ..

HOW MANY MORE CAN YOU DODGE, KYO? ONE? TWO? TWENTY?

...

WHICH BULLET WILL BE YOUR LAST?

I TOLD YOU IT'S FUTILE. YOU'LL NEVER BREAK FREE FROM MY WEB.

STRUGGLE ALL YOU WANT.

NO!
GO TO HELL!
YAAAAAA!
WHAT?

YOU ARE TOO KIND, MAHIRO...
IMPOSSIBLE! HE SNAPPED MY WEB LIKE IT WAS THREAD! PLUS, HE BLOCKED THAT BULLET BY THE HILT OF HIS SWORD!
YOU'RE JUST A STINKING MURDERER ...
YOU KILL WITHOUT MERCY OR THOUGHT. YOU HAVEN'T CHANGED A BIT.

I DO NOT KILL WITHOUT REASON...

WHAT?

I KILL THOSE WHO STAND AGAINST ME. I KILL THOSE WHO WOULD KILL ME.

YOU THINK YOUR KILLING IS JUST?

YOU'VE KILLED EVERYONE WITH GOOD CAUSE, HAVE YOU?

YOU TRULY BELIEVE YOU KILL WITH HONOR?
YOU KILLED MY SISTER, DIDN'T YOU?

WHAT?
...
DO YOU REMEMBER, KYO? FOUR YEARS AGO YOU KILLED MY SISTER...
AND YOU DISAPPEARED WITH OUR FAMILY'S HOLY SWORD.

I COULDN'T FORGIVE YOU. SINCE THEN, I HAVE TRAINED EVERYDAY AT IGA...MY ONLY THOUGHT WAS OF ME SLOWLY KILLING YOU.

THE TRAINING WAS EXCRUCIATINGLY DIFFICULT AND PAINFUL, BUT I WEATHERED IT...

... BECAUSE I LIVED ONLY TO SEE YOU DEAD!

...MY POWERS HAVE COME AT A PRICE... THESE ARE SCARS THAT REMIND ME...
...OF MY HATRED FOR YOU, KYO.
...
I WILL NEVER ...
...NEVER FORGIVE YOU!
TELL ME, KYO!
...
SHE WAS INNOCENT!
WHY ?!

WHY DID YOU KILL MY SISTER ?!
HE'S NOT MOVING !
KYO!
!!

WHAT?
IS THAT WHAT YOU WISH TO BELIEVE?

IS THAT YOUR TRUTH?
THERE ARE MANY TRUTHS, AND WE EACH PICK OUR OWN.

はっ…
ザァァ
MY BROTHER?

I'M SORRY, SIR. MY BROTHER IS AWAY. I DON'T KNOW WHEN HE SHALL RETURN...
WAIT!
I SEE...
MY BROTHER, **MURAMASA**, KEEPS TO HIMSELF MOSTLY. HE...HE MIGHT BE MAKING A SWORD...
...

WHAT'S WRONG, MAHIRO?
ALL THIS RAIN DEPRESSES ME.
AND ...
...HE DOESN'T LEAVE.
PLEASE. EAT.
す!
YOU HAVEN'T EATEN FOR FIVE DAYS. IT'S NOT GOOD FOR YOU TO CARRY ON LIKE THAT.
LEAVE ME ALONE.
I'LL JUST LEAVE IT HERE.
たた…

HEHE. MAHIRO ?
WHAT?
OH... NOTHING!
クス クス
クスー
I SHOULD HAVE NEVER...

I SHOULD HAVE LET YOU STARVE!
...
YOU'VE TAKEN EVERYTHING FROM ME!
THE DAY WE MEET AGAIN, KYO.
ONLY ONE OF US SHALL SEE THE SUNRISE.
DEAL.
...
AH ...

YOU JUST STOOD THERE! SHE COULD'VE KILLED YOU!
And you tore my kimono again!
きぃ~
WHO DO YOU THINK'S GOING TO BUY ME A NEW ONE?
ばっ
LET ME SEE YOUR HAND.
カタ
カタ
IT WAS DELIBER-ATE...

HE HELPED ME BREAK FREE OF MAHIRO'S CONTROL...
BUT IF HE SWUNG ONE HAIR CLOSER...
...I'D BE DEAD.

...
IS HE A MAN?
OR A DEMON WHO SHED HIS HUMANITY LIKE AN OLD SKIN?

チュン
チュン

HOW ARE THE PREPARATIONS?
GOOD.

PLEASE PROCEED AS PLANNED, SAIZO.
YES!

WHAT'S ON YOUR MIND? IS THIS A SOCIAL VISIT, OR DO YOU COME TO FIGHT...

BEAST-SAN?
...

GO AWAY.
jingle

HEY! YOU CAN TALK! SO, HAVE YOU JUST COME TO THREATEN ME?
すっ

I'LL SAY IT AGAIN...

GO AWAY, YUKIMURA SANADA.

jingle

...DON'T YOU THINK IT WOULD LOOK BETTER ON ME?
......!
SO...
jingle
jingle
jingle
WHO SHALL KILL WHOM?
....

MY HAIRPIN! WHEN DID HE...
WHAT?

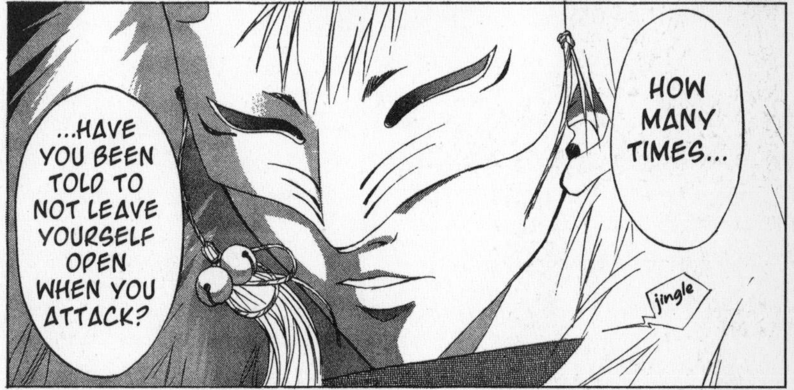
HOW MANY TIMES...
...HAVE YOU BEEN TOLD TO NOT LEAVE YOURSELF OPEN WHEN YOU ATTACK?
jingle

NOW I SUGGEST YOU GO AWAY.
ざっ
は!

......

IEYASU-SAMA...TODAY'S TOURNAMENT HAS COMPLETED. THE LOSERS HAVE BEEN... EXECUTED... AS YOU COMMANDED.
YES. YES. ISN'T THIS A WONDERFUL VIEW, HANZO?
HEH-HEH-HEH. THERE IS ONLY ONE TRUE USE FOR GARBAGE.
SEVEN HAVE ADVANCED ...
PERHAPS SOME OF THEM WILL BE SKILLED IN WAYS WE MIGHT MAKE USE OF.
REGARDLESS...
AND THE WINNERS.
...THE TOKUGAWA HAS NO PLACE FOR TRAITORS.

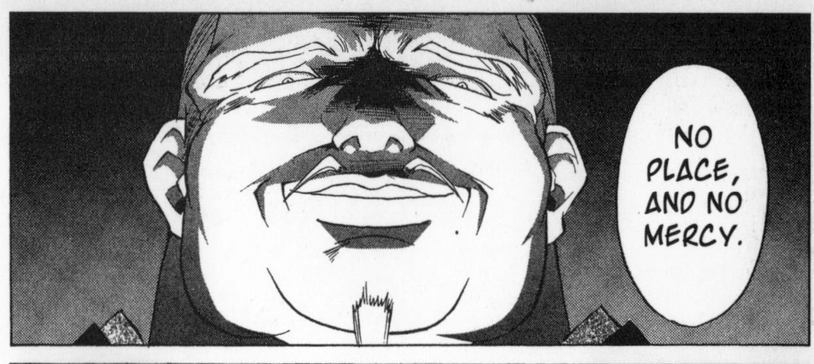
NO PLACE, AND NO MERCY.

LET THEIR FLOWING BLOOD BE A LESSON TO ANY WHO WOULD FOLLOW THEM!

SAMURAI DEEPER KYO

GRAND CHAMPION

MATCHES BEFORE THE SHOGUN

FIRST MATCH: KYO / SHIGEKATA TOGO

SECOND MATCH: YUKINO / JU KAMEN

THIRD MATCH: BENITORA / MOTONAGA SAEKI

FOURTH MATCH: KORETSU / STRONG AR SHICHIR

I DON'T BELIEVE IT!

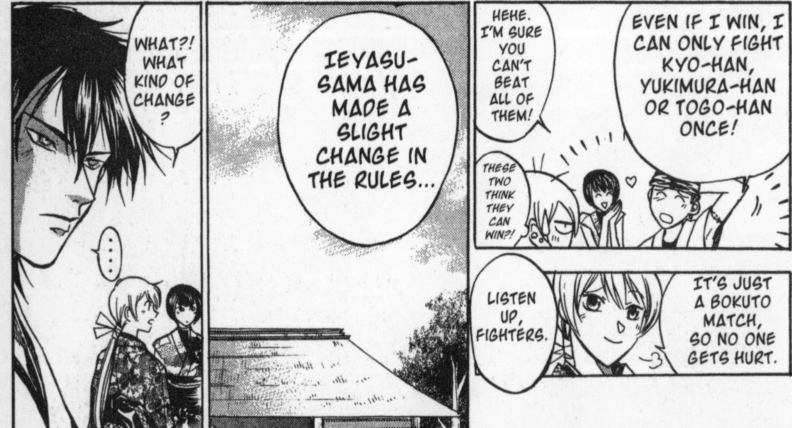

EVEN IF I WIN, I CAN ONLY FIGHT KYO-HAN, YUKIMURA-HAN OR TOGO-HAN ONCE!
HEHE. I'M SURE YOU CAN'T BEAT ALL OF THEM!
THESE TWO THINK THEY CAN WIN?!
IT'S JUST A BOKUTO MATCH, SO NO ONE GETS HURT.
LISTEN UP, FIGHTERS.
IEYASU-SAMA HAS MADE A SLIGHT CHANGE IN THE RULES...
WHAT?! WHAT KIND OF CHANGE?
...

SAMURAI DEEPER
KYO
CHAPTER 29
THE CONTEST OF CHAMPIONS

WHAT?! WE'RE NOT USING A BOKUTO?! REAL SWORDS INSTEAD?

ONE FALSE MOVE AND YOU'RE DEAD.
...

YUYA-HAN? WILL YOU CRY IF I'M KILLED?
WHAT?!
OF COURSE! I HAVEN'T KNOWN YOU LONG, BUT I DO CONSIDER YOU A FRIEND.
Y-YUYA-HAN...
WHAT ABOUT... WHAT IF I FIGHT KYO-HAN...AND I KILL HIM. WHAT THEN?
WHAT?!

I'D MISS YOU MORE THAN I'D MISS YOUR 50 RYO REWARD, BUT KYO'S 1 MILLION IS ANOTHER STORY!
...

IF YOU DO THAT...
...I'LL KILL YOU MYSELF!

WHY ARE THEY USING REAL SWORDS?
SIMPLE. IEYASU-SAMA WANTS US ALL DEAD.

WHAT?!
THE REAL PURPOSE FOR THIS SO-CALLED TOURNAMENT...

...IS TO KILL THOSE WHO WOULD THREATEN THE TOKUGAWA SHOGUNATE.

I DON'T-

THE DOORS HAVE BEEN OPENED TO ALL-COMERS. AND WHY?

IEYASU HAS HIS EYES ON RETIRE-MENT.
HE GROOMS HIS SON TO TAKE HIS PLACE, INSTEAD OF HIDEYORI TOYOTOMI...
BUT FIRST, IEYASU MUST BE CERTAIN THE TOKUGAWA SHOGUNATE IS STABLE.
THE GREAT FIGHTERS WILL COME. THEY WILL COMPETE.
THEY WILL DIE.

AND THOSE THREE HITMEN FROM HIS RIVAL CLANS, MORI, UESUGI AND DATE WILL UNKNOWINGLY SWEEP UP THE TRASH.

AND NOW, WE ARE THREE MORE RATS IN HIS TRAP.

IT'S ALL SO MORBID, ISN'T IT?

KYA HA HA

...

YOU KNOW ALL THIS, AND YET YOU STILL COME? I WONDER WHO HAS THE GREATER PLAN?

I'LL TAKE THAT AS A COMPLIMENT.

WELL, YUKIMURA'S PLAN IS OBVIOUS, TOO...

PERHAPS. BUT DO NOT UNDERESTIMATE HIS MIND.

...

I HAVE ANOTHER PLAN PREPARED.

LET THEM CUT FLESH AND BREAK BONES...

...AND WE SHALL SEE WHOSE BLOW TOPPLES THE SHOGUNATE.

....

....

YOU DELIVER IEYASU'S HEAD AND LET ME WORRY ABOUT THE OTHERS.
tha-thump
THIS IS GETTING INTER-ESTING..
ba-dump

thump-thump
SOMETHING'S AMISS...
I HAVE SUCH A BAD FEELING ABOUT THIS...

A VERY, VERY BAD FEELING.
LET THE TOURNAMENT BEGIN!

KYO-DONO VS. SHIGEKATA-DONO!
YUKINO-DONO VS. BEAST KAMEN-DONO!
BENITORA-DONO VS. MOTONAGA-DONO!
KORETSU-DONO VS. SHICHIRO UEMON-DONO!
pitter
pitter
LET'S MAKE THIS A FAIR FIGHT!

A FIVE-SHAKU SWORD... YIN-YANG CREST ON HIS BACK...
AND THOSE EYES... RED LIKE A DEMON'S ...

KYO-DONO ...
YOU SHARE THE NAME OF A LEGEND...

PERHAPS I AM THE LEGEND.

I HOPE SO. I'VE WANTED TO FACE DEMON EYES KYO...

TO TEST MY **JIGEN-STYLE** SKILLS...

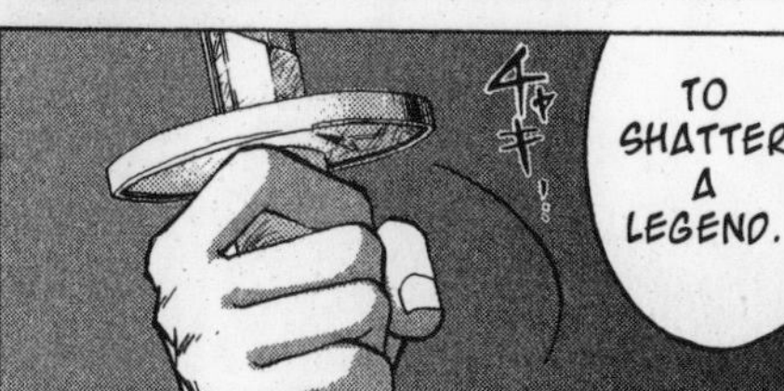

TO SHATTER A LEGEND.

SO TELL ME KYO, DO I LOOK LIKE A LEGEND KILLER?
COME FEEL THE BLADE OF SELF-KNOWING... AND MAKE ME FAMOUS!
I DON'T KNOW ANYTHING ABOUT YOUR SELF-KNOWING, OR WHATEVER...
INTER-ESTING ...
COME ON...
THIS'LL BE FUN.
HIS EYES! THEY'RE... GLOWING!

オ
オ
ジリ
ジリ
オ
オ
オ
ろ…!
ザァ

CHE SU TOH!
KYO!

YOU...YOU BARELY MOVED! BUT HOW-?!
DO YOU KNOW HITOTACHI NO UCHI...
...THE ABILITY TO KILL WITH BLINDING SPEED ON THE FIRST STRIKE?
IT'S ALSO CALLED THE DRAGONFLY STYLE, DUE TO THE DISTINCTIVE WAY ONE HOLDS HIS SWORD. YOU PUT ALL YOUR STRENGTH INTO THE FIRST STRIKE AND BISECT THE ENEMY WITH A DOWNWARD DIAGONAL SLICE.
YOU DON'T THINK ABOUT DEFENSE OR THE SECOND STRIKE. IT'S A FURIOUS SWORD TECHNIQUE WITH A SINGLE DEADLY STRIKE.
HE CAN SLICE KYO IN HALF WITH ONE BLOW!
THAT BLOW WAS MERELY A TEST TO DRAW YOU OUT...

I HAVE SEEN YOUR TRUE SPEED.
NOW...
I SHALL SHOW YOU MINE...

LET ME ASK YOU SOMETHING...
DID YOU SEE ME MOVE?
WHAT DOES THAT MATTER?
IF YOU CANNOT SEE ME MOVE...
...HOW CAN YOU KILL ME?

ONE STRIKE...
WHAT?
SHUT UP!
THIS IS THE END!
GO TO HELL, DEMON EYES KYO!
FIFTY. YOU CANNOT KILL ME.

I TOLD YOU TO LEAVE.
I'VE NEVER BEEN A GOOD LISTENER.
WELL, THEN ...
DIE!
SECRET DEATH BLADE!

TENCHI GENEI-KEN!
THE SWORD OF HEAVEN AND EARTH'S ILLUSIONS!
WHAT?!

IT LOOKS LIKE YOU MISSED.
YOU BROKE THE ILLUSION! HOW?!
A FITTING NAME... SWORD OF ILLUSION.
Just like the old proverb.
IT'S SO EASY TO FOOL THE EYES.
BUT THE TRICK DOESN'T WORK IF MY EYES ARE CLOSED.
HAHAHA! YOU LOOK SUR-PRISED...
A BLUR OF IMAGES... THE REAL SWORD CAN BE UP, DOWN, LEFT...?

I KNOW YOU TOO WELL.
IT'S ALWAYS YOUR FIRST LINE OF ATTACK.
DID YOU THINK I WOULDN'T KNOW YOU?
IT'S BEEN A LONG TIME...
... NOBUYUKI SANADA... MY BROTHER.

SAMURAI DEEPER KYO
clink
THE WINNER: BENI-TORA-DONO!
I WONDER HOW KYO-HAN AND YUKIMURA-HAN ARE FAIRING...
TOO EASY.
HMMM...

IT'S BEEN A WHILE.
I DIDN'T THINK THAT I COULD FOOL YOU UNTIL THE VERY END.
Jingle
YOU'RE ABSOLUTE-LY RIGHT...
....

SAMURAI DEEPER
KYO
CHAPTER 30
LOYALTY AND PRIDE
YES, HOW COULD I NOT KNOW MY OWN BROTHER?
HUH?
WHAT?!

HOLY SHIT! HE LOOKS EXACTLY LIKE...

... YUKI-MURA-HAN!

AND YOU STILL LOOK LIKE A LITTLE BOY, BROTHER.

WHAT ARE YOU DOING HERE? YOU SHOULD BE OLD ENOUGH TO KNOW BETTER.

YOU SHOULD BE ASHAMED! THE OLDEST BROTHER OF THE SANADA FAMILY HELPING TOKUGAWA?!

YOUR WORDS ARE AS MEANINGLESS AS A CHATTERING MONKEY.

...

YOU'VE FORSAKEN THE FAMILY NAME. AND FOR WHAT REASON?
TO BE A BETTER LAP DOG TO TOKU-GAWA?!
WHY, BROTHER? WHY HAVE YOU DISHONORED OUR FATHER'S NAME?
I AM NO LONGER YOUR BROTHER.
...
GIVE UP NOW, YUKI-MURA.
THIS IS YOUR FINAL CHANCE.
IF OUR ROLES WERE REVERSED ...
... WOULD YOU DO WHAT YOU ARE ASKING OF ME?
NO.
I SUP-POSE NOT.
SHOW ME, BROTHER... SHOW ME HOW WELL YOU WIELD THE KATANA!

ざぁぁ...
WHAT DID YOU SAY, DEMON EYES KYO?
ARE YOU DEAF AS WELL AS SLOW?
HOW CAN YOU EVER DEFEAT ...

...WHAT YOU CANNOT HIT?

ENOUGH OF YOUR BABBLE! SHOW ME YOUR TRUE POWER!
CHE SU TOH!
GO TO HELL, DEMON EYES!
HE'S EVEN FASTER THAN BEFORE!
AND DEADLIER!

UGH!
YOU'RE JOKING, RIGHT? YOU MOVE SLOWER THAN AN OLD WOMAN!
NOW TASTE THE SPEED OF WING CUTTER!
DIE!
KYO!

WHAT MAKES YOU THINK...

...I WAS EVEN TRYING TO MOVE?

When I move, you'll know it.

HE...HE BLOCKED THE ATTACK WITH THE TIP OF HIS SWORD!

THE ACCURACY... AMAZING!

UGH...
UGH...

YOU'RE NOT EVEN GOOD ENOUGH FOR ME TO KILL.

BUT... I WILL SHOW YOU SOME-THING... GREAT.

WIND OF GOD, SWORD OF DEATH.
UGH.
HIS POWER... IT'S GROWING! I CAN FEEL IT!

MI ZU CHI!
WHAT?! IT FELT LIKE THE WIND JUST WENT THROUGH MY BODY!
AH... GUH...

GUAAAAAAH!

UGH!
THE SWORD...
IT SLICED HIM LIKE PAPER IN ONE ATTACK!
"MIZUCHI?" WHAT DOES IT EVEN MEAN?
I'LL FORGIVE YOUR ARROGANCE. BUT ONLY THIS ONE TIME.
YOUR SWORD! WHAT IN THE WORLD DID YOU-
NOTHING IN THIS WORLD.
DID YOU HEAR IT, TOO?
THE SOUND OF DIVINE WIND...
...
LONG AGO...
...MY MASTER TAUGHT ME THE FOUR ELEMENTS OF SWORD SKILL...
EYES. FEET. ZEN. POWER.

WHEN HE TOLD ME THIS, I HARDLY UNDERSTOOD, BUT NOW...
A SWORD MIGHT AS WELL BE A FAN, IF YOU CANNOT HIT THE ENEMY.
HE WAS MOVING!
I JUST COULDN'T SEE IT.
UGH!
THIS MAN...
HE IS TRULY...
...THE LEGENDARY DEMON EYES KYO!
I... LOST...

......
TIGER!
HEY, YUYA-HAN.

I'M SO HAPPY YOU WON!
AH! IT WAS EASY!
But more praise, please!
HOW IS YUKIMURA-SAN FARING?
UH ...
WELL ...
ギィン
ギン
WHAT?

ギリ
WHAT! THEY LOOK THE SAME! HOW-
HE'S YUKIMURA-HAN'S OLDER BROTHER.
WHAT?!
NOBUYUKI SANADA. THEY SAY HE'S AS GREAT A SAMURAI AS YUKIMURA-HAN.

THEIR POWER IS EQUAL, BUT THEIR STYLES COULDN'T BE MORE DIFFERENT. YUKIMURA-HAN IS FLEXIBLE AND NOBUYUKI IS TOUGH AS STEEL.
IT WAS THESE TWO BROTHERS THAT MADE THE SANADA HOUSE UNCONQUER-ABLE.

BUT WHY ARE THEY FIGHT-ING?
I DUNNO. BUT I'VE HEARD NOBUYUKI ABANDONED HIS FATHER AND BROTHER AND TOOK SIDES WITH TOKUGAWA AT SEKIGAHARA.
THERE'S EVEN A RUMOR THAT NOBUYUKI HAS GROWN TO BE IEYASU'S MOST TRUSTED SAMURAI.
...

SO SAD...

TWO BROTHERS FIGHTING EACH OTHER.
SUCH A TERRIBLE FATE.
AND SAD... SO SAD.
...
ALTHOUGH ...

NOBUYUKI IS A MEANS TO AN END. ONE WHO MAY BETRAY EVEN ME.
IF HE DIES TODAY, I HAVE NO REAL PAIN.
THE TOKUGAWA SHOGUNATE HAS NO NEED FOR SANADA BLOOD.
INDEED, IT WOULD SERVE ME BEST IF THEY BOTH DIED.
YOU'VE HARDENED, YUKIMURA.
THANKS. YOUR SKILL IS GREAT AS WELL, BROTHER.
WHY DO YOU WASTE IT IN THE NAME OF TOKUGAWA?
YOUR THOUGHTS ARE LOST TO ME.
PERHAPS I CAN OFFER YOU SOME... ENLIGHTENMENT.
...

YUKI-MURA...
...NO MATTER HOW GOOD YOU ARE, YOU CANNOT WIN.
THEY SAY YOU'RE THE SMARTEST SAMURAI IN THE LAND? YET, ALL YOU'VE EVER LED ARE LOSERS.
...
AND YOUR STYLE...
...IS ONE OF DEFENSE, NOT OFFENSE.
YOU CANNOT DEFEAT ME BECAUSE YOU'VE NEVER KNOWN VICTORY...
... BROTHER.
HEH-HEH-HEH...
WHAT YOU SAY WAS ALL VERY TRUE.
LONG AGO.

COME, BROTHER! COME NOW AND SEE IF I KNOW VICTORY!
ざくあっ
....
HAAAA!

GO, YUKIMURA-SAN! YOU CAN DO IT!
IMPOS-SIBLE.
YEAH...
...
WHAT?!
WITHOUT DOUBT...
...YUKIMURA WOULD LOSE THIS MATCH 8-OUT-OF-10 TIMES.
WHY?!
IT LOOKS LIKE HE'S WINNING!
HOW CAN HE LOSE?
huff huff

huff
huff
HE WILL LOSE, BECAUSE HE HAS NO CHANCE OF WINNING...
ザ
...
huff
IF HE KEEPS FIGHTING THIS WAY...
huff huff

...YUKIMURA WOULD LOSE THIS MATCH 8-OUT-OF-10 TIMES...
...
huff huff
huff
IF HE KEEPS FIGHTING THIS WAY...
huff
huff huff
SAMURAI DEEPER KYO
CHAPTER 31 A WINNER'S PRAISE

GUH!
IS THIS YOUR "WINNING" SKILL, YUKIMURA?
YOU CAN'T EVEN REACH ME!
ugh
DO YOU KNOW WHY?
...
WE BOTH TRAINED UNDER OUR FATHER. ALL THAT YOU KNOW, I KNEW FIRST.
BUT IT'S MORE THAN THAT, BROTHER.
YOU FIGHT TO **NOT LOSE**...
huff huff
WHERE IS THERE HOPE FOR VICTORY IN THAT?!
WHAT THE HELL IS HE TALKING ABOUT?!
Uh... that hurts.
IF YOU FIGHT TO NOT LOSE, THEN YOU WIN? Right?!
I KNOW IT'S CONFUSING, BUT TO NOT LOSE IS DIFFERENT THAN WINNING.
WHAT?!

TO WIN, YOU HAVE TO **FIGHT TO WIN**. YET, IF THE OPPONENTS ARE EQUAL, THEN YOU MUST HAVE SOMETHING MORE THAN SKILL.
CALL IT LUCK, OR A GAMBLE, BUT YOU MUST FEEL THE FLOW OF THE MATCH, AND WAIT FOR THE PERFECT MOMENT TO RISK EVERYTHING TO WIN.
UGH!
ONE WHO FIGHTS TO NOT LOSE, WILL NEVER TAKE THAT RISK.
AND SO, IF THE OPPONENTS ARE EQUAL, TO BREAK THAT BALANCE, A RISK **MUST** BE TAKEN.
THAT'S WHY THE STYLE OF FIGHTING TO NOT LOSE IS NOT THE SWORD OF VICTORY.
...
THE MIND THAT DOES NOT GAMBLE IS EASY TO READ.
GRADUALLY, YOU WILL SEE ALL HIS MOVES.
THE KILLING GAME SHOWS NO KINDNESS TO THE COWARD WHO AVOIDS CHANCE.
pant pant huff
SUCH A SHAME. YOU HAVE TREMEN-DOUS SKILL.
...
BUT DON'T WORRY ...
huff pant

...I SHALL REUNITE YOU WITH FATHER AND OUR FAMILY...
...IN THE GRAVES AT MOUNT KUDO.
huff huff
....!
huff huff
LOOK AT HIS EYES. HE'S SERIOUS.
WHAT?!
....
K...
YOU CAN'T JUST STAND THERE, KYO!
YOU'VE GOT TO STOP THIS!
THE FINAL CHAPTER HAS BEEN WRITTEN.
HEH-HEH-HEH. HURRY NOW...
LET'S SEE SOME BLOOD.

FAREWELL...
...MY BROTHER.
KYO! PLEASE!
...
FARE-WELL!
IF ONLY...
...KYO-SHIRO WERE HERE!
NOOOOO!
ポタ
ポタ
ポタ

I CANNOT ALLOW ANYONE TO HARM YUKIMURA-SAMA.

EVEN YOU, NOBUYUKI-SAMA.

S... SAIZO ...

I WOULD DIE BEFORE LETTING THIS SWORD...
... TOUCH YUKI-MURA-SAMA!
YOU ARE AGAINST ME, DESPITE THE FACT THAT MY OPPONENT IS A PUPPET OF THE SANADA FAMILY?
I WON'T RESIST YOU, BUT NEITHER WILL I LET YOU KILL YUKIMURA-SAMA. PLEASE PUT YOUR SWORD BACK INTO YOUR SHEATH.
....

I COULD NEVER HARM SUCH HONOR.
NEVER.

ODD. YOU COULD HAVE STRUCK ME DOWN WHEN SAIZO STOPPED MY BLADE.

YOU ARE TOO SENTI-MENTAL.

チャキ!

SUCH KINDNESS IS THE DEATH OF A SAMURAI.

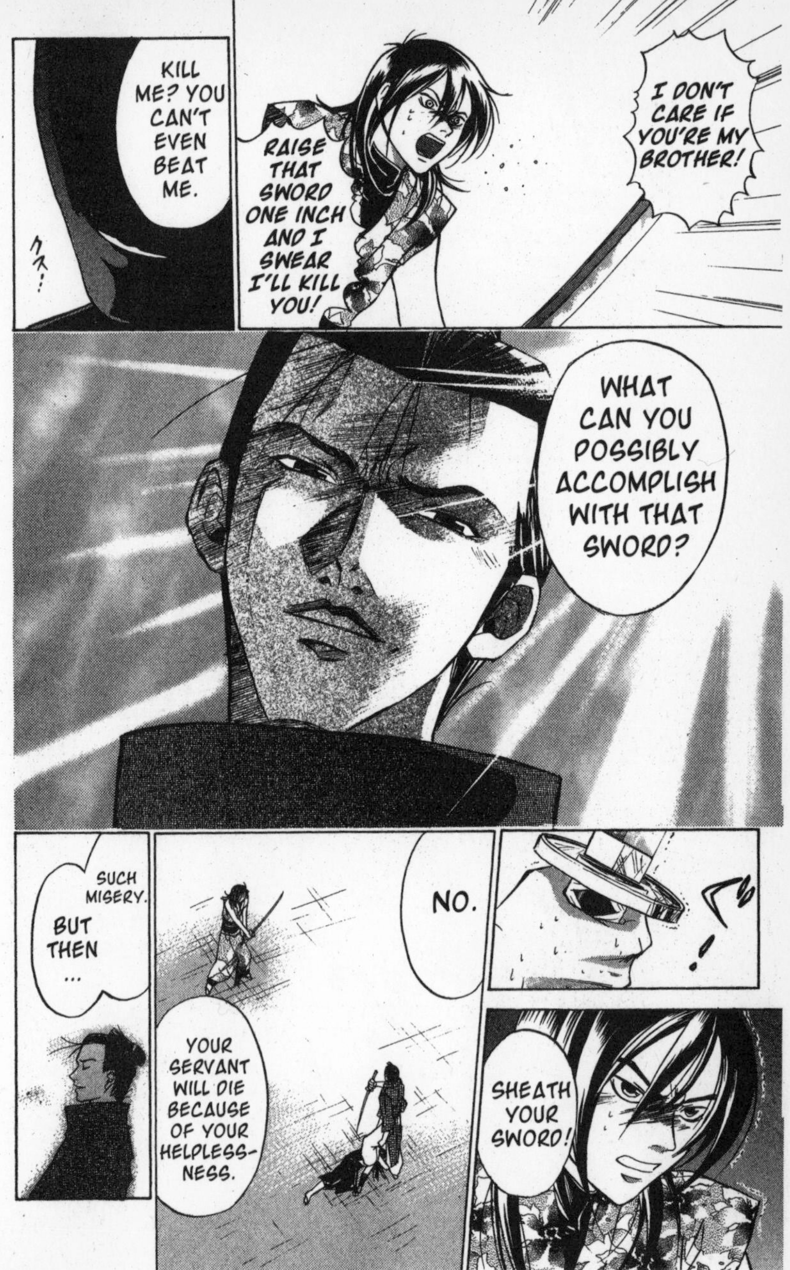
I DON'T CARE IF YOU'RE MY BROTHER!
RAISE THAT SWORD ONE INCH AND I SWEAR I'LL KILL YOU!
KILL ME? YOU CAN'T EVEN BEAT ME.
WHAT CAN YOU POSSIBLY ACCOMPLISH WITH THAT SWORD?
NO.
SUCH MISERY.
BUT THEN ...
SHEATH YOUR SWORD!
YOUR SERVANT WILL DIE BECAUSE OF YOUR HELPLESS-NESS.

...A FOOL SERVANT FOR A FOOL SAMURAI.

FOOL SERVANT...

YOU WON'T MISS HIM LONG.

IN FACT, YOU'LL BE JOINING HIM.

WHO IS...

...THE FOOL?
WHAT?!
WHERE DID YOU... WHERE DID YOU GET THAT POWER?!
ARE YOU OKAY, SAIZO?
YUKI-MURA-SAMA... I AM SORRY...
HOLD ON, SAIZO. I WON'T BE LONG.
....
YOU CAN SLANDER ME AS MUCH AS YOU WANT.
BUT...

...YOU'VE GONE TOO FAR...
...BROTHER.
YUKI ...
YUKI-MURA-SA...
....
STUPID.
NOW HE FINALLY GETS SERIOUS.
Too little, too late.

WHAT ARE YOU WAITING FOR, NOBUYUKI?!
KILL HIM!
I COMMAND YOU!
...

...
NOBU ...
DAMMIT! I DON'T CARE ANYMORE!
KILL THEM! KILL THEM ALL!

COME OUT!
!?

WHAT?
A MILITIA!
And samurai!
SO. HE'S PLAYED HIS HAND.
GREAT FIGHTERS! SKILLED SWORDSMEN! WARRIORS!
BAH! YOU ARE ALL JUST PAWNS!
HEH-HEH-HEH.
I CANNOT ALLOW YOU TO LEAVE HERE ALIVE.
....

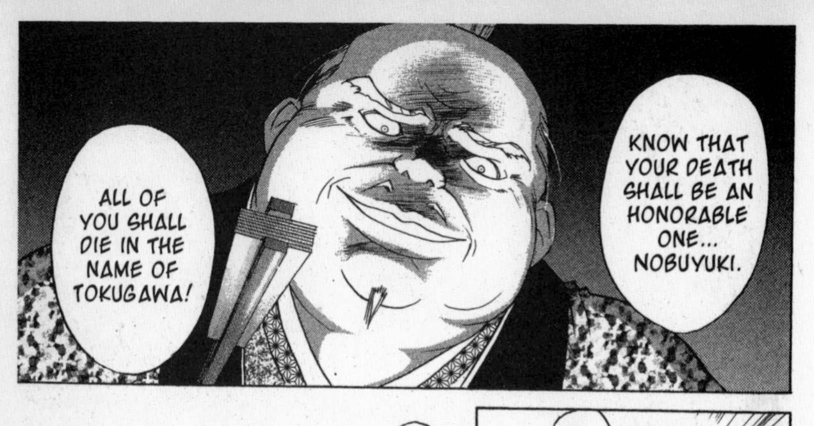
KNOW THAT YOUR DEATH SHALL BE AN HONORABLE ONE... NOBUYUKI.
ALL OF YOU SHALL DIE IN THE NAME OF TOKUGAWA!

HEH-HEH-HEH.
UGLY.

YOU LOOK SO DAMN UGLY...
...WHEN YOU LAUGH.

WHAT?
...
WHAT DID YOU SAY?

I SEE. YOU'D LIKE TO DIE FIRST?
PIKU PIKU
SO BE IT.

YOUR BLOOD WILL BE THE FIRST TO WET THE GROUND.
...

FIRE!

OH, IEYASU...
...YOU'RE SUCH A PIG.
WHAT?

GUH!
WHAT THE HELL ARE YOU WAITING FOR?!
SAMURAI ATTACK!
!?

WHAT?!
ARE YOU SURE THOSE WERE SAMURAI?
Clack
I THINK SOMEONE'S PLAYED A JOKE ON YOU.
I...
ゴク
WHAT... AH... AH...

WHO THE HELL DO YOU THINK YOU ARE?!
WHY DO YOU FIGHT AGAINST ME?
ALL OF THIS REALLY...
...PISSES ME OFF!
...
YOU PLOT AGAINST ME!
OPPOSE ME!
SHUT YOUR FAT MOUTH.

SHUT UP AND GET READY...
...TO DIE.

Kamijyo Circumstances

The Mystery of Kyo

At H-shi's desk, anyone can look over from the other side.

Actually, H-shi came up with the name **"Samurai Deeper Kyo."**
ALL RIGHT! IT'S DONE!
YEAH.
Samurai Deeper Kyo

One day, shortly after the series was first being published...
WHAT DOES THE "DEEPER" PART MEAN?
I ASKED H-SHI ABOUT IT, BUT HE WOULDN'T TELL ME. HE JUST SMILED.
DID HE TELL YOU, KAMIJYO?
HUH?
Their favorite color is orange.

HEH-HEH-HEH... IT MEANS ...
I know that because I am the author.
DEEP!

...
...
WE ALREADY KNOW THAT!
OH.

IN TRUTH, IT MEANS A DEEP PERSON. **"SAMURAI DEEPER"** MEANS A DEEP PERSON WHO HAS MASTERED THE ART OF SAMURAI. IN SHORT, IT'S SAMURAI OTAKU.

I understood it, I just can't explain it well. Still, H-shi is smiling. Maybe there is a hidden meaning...

HEY, EVERYBODY! IT'S ME, YUKIMURA. I GOT MORE VALENTINE'S DAY CHOCOLATE THAN ANYBODY! I TRIED TO SHARE MY CHOCOLATES WITH KYO-SAN (MAIN CHARACTER), WHO DIDN'T EVEN RECEIVE ANY! I ATE AND ATE AND ATE...
...
Thanks even to Kamijyo! I ate and ate and ate...
Yuya-han? Do you have one for me?
CHOCOLA

Hi. Kamijyo here. How is everyone? Volume #4 was published without a hitch thanks to everyone who cheered me up in so many ways. Thank you very much for all the cheerful postcards, letters to "Question Corner," and all the terrific illustrations. I'm reading each one carefully because your opinions are important to me- they're like treasures!

I cannot reply to all the letters (I made postcards, though) and there's not enough room to publish all the illustrations. At the Question Corner, we receive many inquiries about the characters and even me! Although, most are about the characters. (I thought that'd be the case.) Starting with this volume, we'll be printing character profiles. You'll find the secrets of your favorite characters and even some hints to the mystery of the story.

So, are you getting excited? Great! Yes! See you again at the end of the next volume!

\- Akimine.

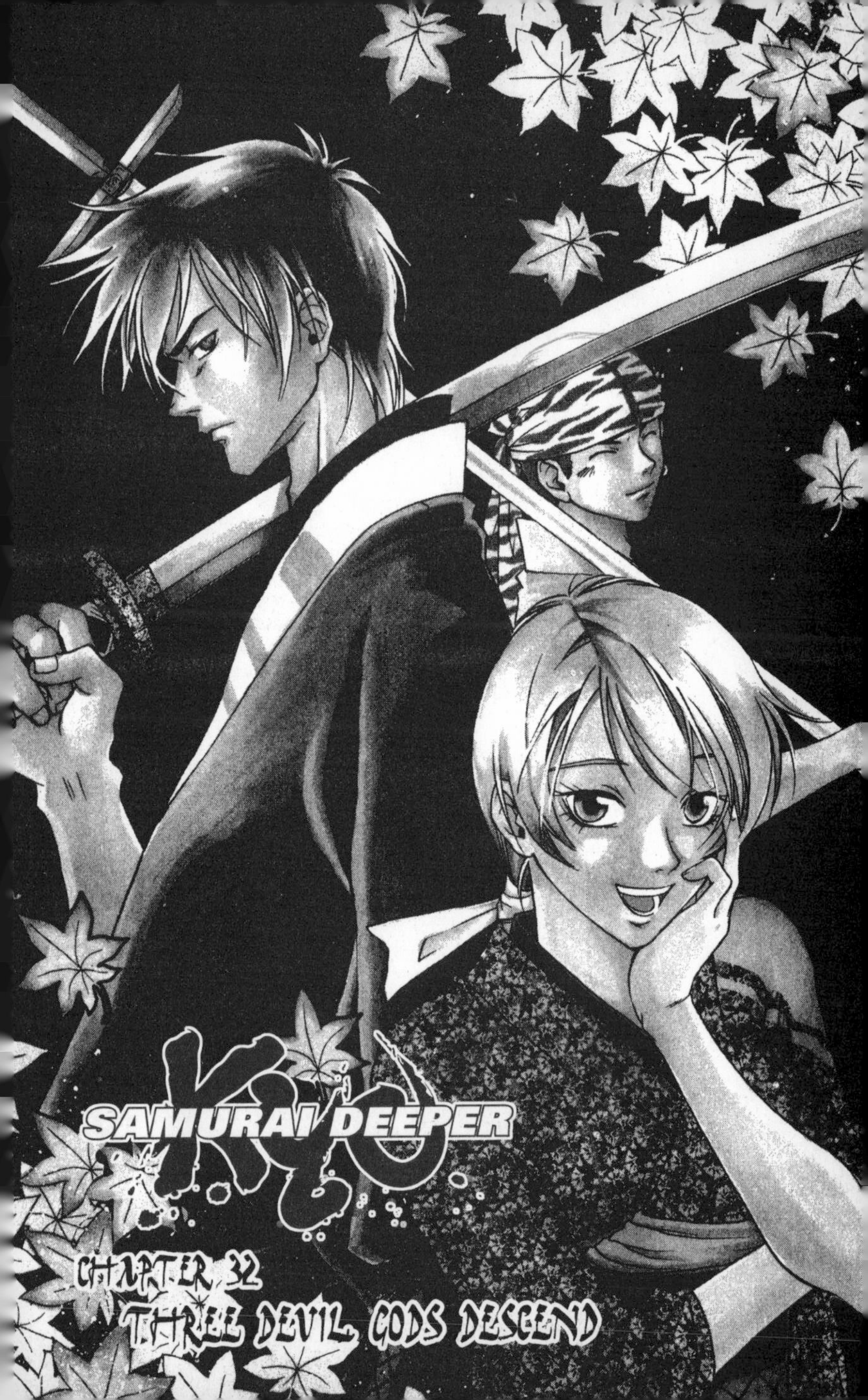
SAMURAI DEEPER
KYO
CHAPTER 32
THREE DEVIL GODS DESCEND

SHUT UP AND GET READY TO DIE.
SHIT!
YOU ARRO-GANT...
EVERYBODY! EVERYBODY! COME OUT!

HEH-HEH-HEH. WHERE ARE YOUR BOASTS NOW? NOT SO EASY, IS IT?
More than a hundred men.
IEYASU-HAN'S GOT HIMSELF A REAL NICE FORCE.
YEAH.
WHAT THE HELL CAN THREE OF THEM DO AGAINST THIS?
WHATTA PAIN.
HEH-HEH-HEH. ARE YOU SCARED TO DIE?
LET'S SEE...

IT'S ABOUT 30-TO-1.
TOO BAD THEY'RE JUST PLAIN SOLDIERS.
IT'S REALLY NOT WORTH THE EFFORT.
W-WHAT?!
HUH?
HEY! GIRL!

W... WHAT?
GET LOST. YOU'LL SLOW US DOWN.
Did I startle you?
WHAT?!
THEN I SUGGEST YOU STAY CLOSE.
WHAT DID YOU SAY?!
MIND YOUR OWN DAMN BUSINESS!
FINE!
HUH?
COME ON! NOW!
Y... YES!
ENOUGH! KILL THEM ALL!

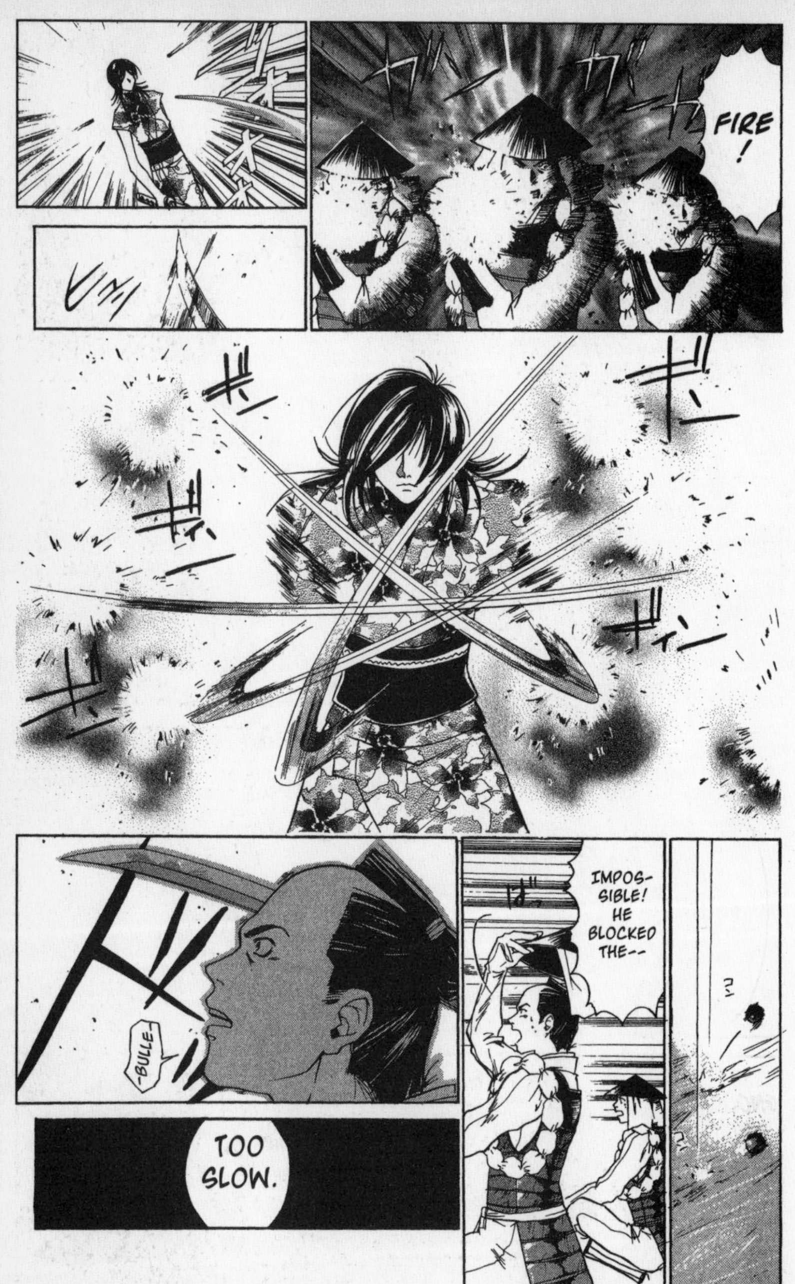
FIRE!
IMPOSSIBLE! HE BLOCKED THE--
-BULLE-
TOO SLOW.

BULLETS CAN'T STOP ME.
Guh!
HA AAA!
OOPS.
I WENT A LITTLE TOO FAR.
And I made a little mess.
GO TO HELL, IDIOT!
WHAT? WHERE'D HE GO?
WHAT'RE YOU DOING? I'M RIGHT HERE!

!!!
And here.
They look surprised.
Haha haha!
Sur-prised?
Hello! Hello!

...TIME TO DIE.

WHAT THE HELL?!
AEEE!!!

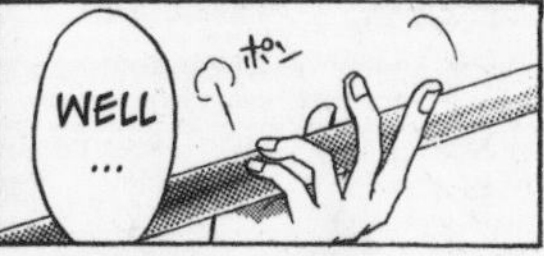
WELL ...

UH ...
...
HEH... EH...

GUH...
WHAT'S WRONG? COME ON, COWARDS!
WAIT...
WHY ARE YOU PROVOKING THEM? IF THEY ALL FIRE AT ONCE, WE'LL BE KILLED!
HOW MANY BULLETS CAN YOU DODGE?

UH... UHHH...
ALL OF THEM.

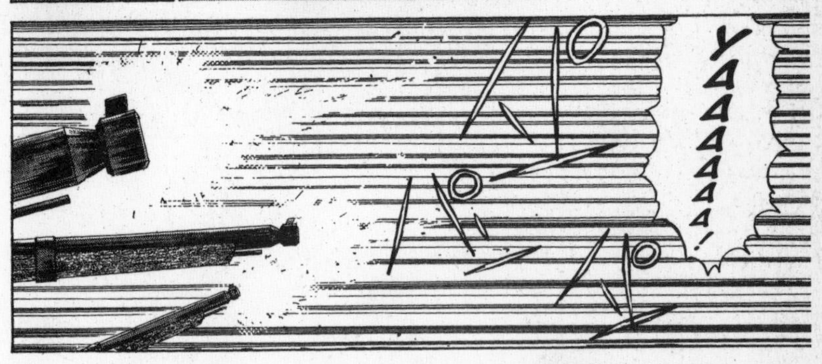
YAAAAAA!

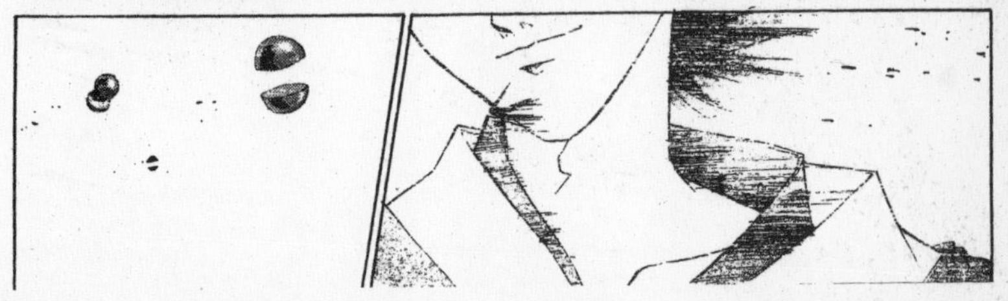

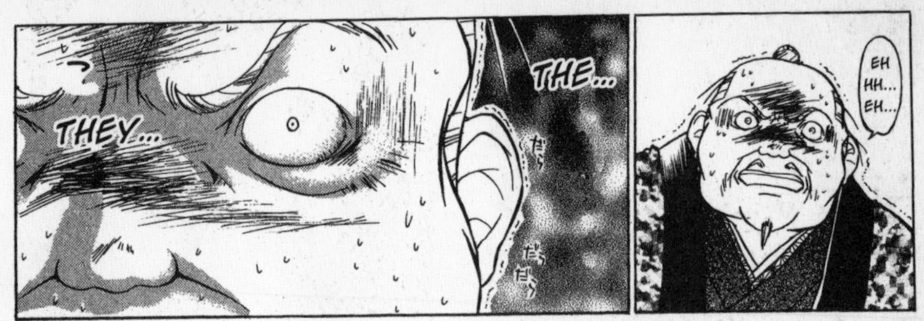
EH HH... EH...
THE...
THEY...

THEY AREN'T HUMAN!

THEY'RE MONSTERS!

AND WHERE ARE YOU GOING?

YOU CAN'T RUN FROM ME.
YAAAAAAAH!
PLEASE FORGIVE ME, YUKIMURA!
I'LL GIVE YOU 100,000-NO! 200,000! ANYTHING! PLEASE, YUKIMURA!
DON'T HURT ME!
IS IT LIFE YOU WANT SO BADLY, IEYASU?
IF YOU DON'T WANT TO DIE...
...THEN DON'T BEG ME TO SPARE YOU. BEG...
... ENMA, THE KING OF HELL!
GYAAAAH!

GUH! GUH!
OPEN YOUR EYES, OR DIE IN VAIN.
YOU'RE BEGINNING TO BORE ME, BROTHER.
WELL DONE, NOBUYUKI! I'LL LEAVE THIS TO YOU!
...
YOU FOLLOW YOUR PATH, AND I WALK UPON MINE.
HEH-HEH-HEH. SO BE IT.
OKAY.
WELL?

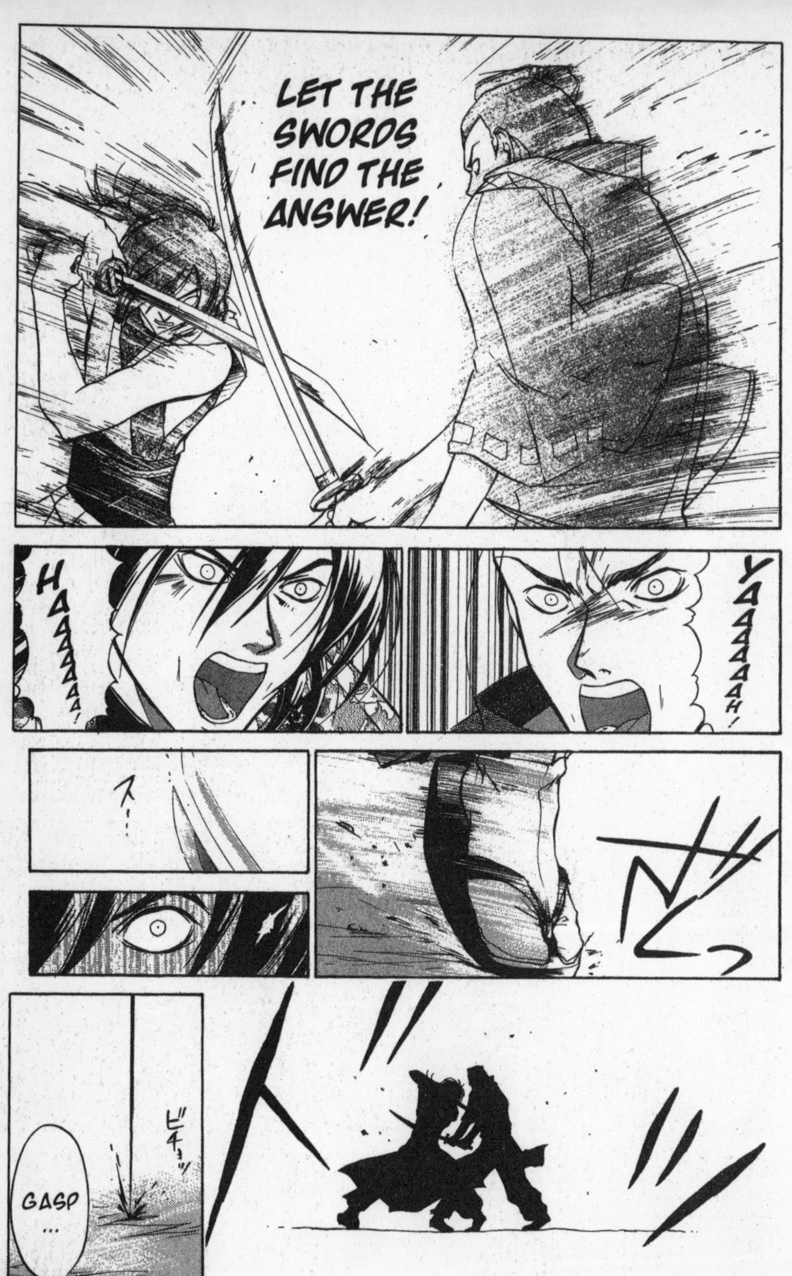
LET THE SWORDS FIND THE ANSWER!
YAAAAAAH!
HAAAAAAA!
GASP ...

YOU'VE GROWN STRONG, YUKIMURA...

GUH!
WHY?
WHY DID YOU STAY YOUR SWORD?
GUH GUH
AT THE LAST MOMENT...YOU ALSO AVOIDED THE KILLING BLOW. SO SENTIMENTAL...
GUH... GUH...
BUT...
WITH THIS, I HAVE NOTHING LEFT TO TEACH YOU.
.....!?
FORGIVE ME, YUKI-MURA...

FATHER... FATHER AND I HAD A PLAN...
TOKUGAWA. TOYOTOMI. ONLY ONE SIDE COULD SURVIVE SEKIGAHARA. OUR FAMILY WAS STRONG, BUT IT DIDN'T MATTER.
TOKUGAWA. TOYOTOMI. WHO WON DID NOT MATTER. IT WAS THE SANADA BLOODLINE I SOUGHT TO PROTECT. YOU HAD CHOSEN TOYOTOMI. I SIDED WITH TOKUGAWA.
THUS, NO MATTER WHO WON, A SANADA WOULD STAND AT HIS SIDE IN THE NEW ORDER. OUR FAMILY WOULD SURVIVE.
....
I AM SORRY TO HAVE KEPT THIS A SECRET, BUT AS THEY SAY, "TO DECEIVE AN ENEMY, DECEIVE YOUR ALLIES FIRST..."
BESIDES, IF YOU KNEW, YOU WOULD HAVE NEVER FOUGHT ME.
THOUGH IT PAINED ME, TOKUGAWA COULD NOT DOUBT.
BUT...
...YOUR SENTIMENT WAS STRONGER THAN YOUR BLADE.
I WILL UNDER-STAND YOUR ANGER...
Shall we finish what we started?
....

YOU HAVE SUCH STRENGTH. YOU'LL BE OKAY...
YUKI...
I AM... PLEASED THAT YOU STILL CARE, BUT MY HAND IS DEALT...
HEH-HEH-HEH.
I WAS BORN WITH THIS PERSONALITY. I CAN'T CHANGE SO EASILY.
... BIG BROTHER.

THERE IS NO FIGURING YOU...
YES!
SIGH...
YOU BETTER TEND THAT WOUND...
Or you will be dead.
I HAVE TO FIND IEYASU.
WAIT...
THE SAMURAI... THE TERRIBLE ONE...HAS GONE AFTER HIM...
YUKIMURA... THERE IS SOMETHING I MUST TELL YOU ABOUT HIM...
WHAT...?

どす!!
huff
pant
どす
どす
huff
wheeze
pant
I'M... I'M SAFE...
huff
はあ
はあ
THOSE BASTARDS! I WON'T FORGET THIS! I'LL BRING MY ARMY!
I'VE GOT TO GET BACK TO THE CASTLE...
I CAN'T LET YOU DO THAT.
WHAT?!
YOU'LL DIE HERE.
I... I...
IT'S NOTHING PERSONAL AGAINST YOU. I JUST HAVE A JOB TO DO...
AH ...
BUT FIRST ...

...TELL ME WHERE IEYASU IS.
WHAT?
WHAT ARE YOU SAYING?! I'M IEYASU!
I'M NOT ASKING ABOUT YOU.
NOW YOU'RE GOING TO TELL ME...
ス!
...WHERE THE REAL IEYASU IS!

STAFF

Yuzu Haruno
(The Chief of Staff)
Hazuki Asami
Kenichi Suetake
Takaya Nagao
Note: In order of coming on staff
Sho Yashioka
(Until chapter 31)
Yuuji Takada
(Chapter 29)

I WANT TO THANK THE WHOLE STAFF FOR DOING SUCH A GREAT JOB. ALSO, MR. H AND MR. S FOR WATCHING OVER KYO. MR. I, WHO LEFT AFTER VOLUME 3 AND MR. Y WHO STARTED WITH VOLUME 4. AND THEN THERE'S THE PEOPLE IN THE SALES DEPARTMENT, PEOPLE WHO WORK PART-TIME AND PEOPLE WHO LAY IN THE SCREEN TONES, ETC. AND THANKS TO THE PEOPLE AT THE PUBLISHER AND THE PRINTING COMPANY, MR. K AND SENSEI A., WHO GAVE ME ADVICE, MY FRIENDS WHO BUY MORE ISSUES TO INCREASE SALES (HAHA!) AND EVERYONE ELSE WHO WORKS IN MANGA. I APPRECIATE ALL THE READERS. I WORK HARD TO DO MY BEST.

CHARACTER PROFILE

Well, please introduce yourself.
I'M KYOSHIRO MIBU. I'M A MALE, 20 YEARS OLD, 5'9," 65KG, BLOOD TYPE AB. I'M A MEDICINE SELLER FOR LOVE AND PEACE! WOULD YOU LIKE MY SPECIAL RECIPE?

No thank you. You said your hobby is sleeping and your strongest skill is eating...
EXACTLY! AND MAKING SECRET MEDICINE, TOO. I'M GOOD AT IT!

I see. What's some of your favorite things?
SAVING PEOPLE AND WOMEN! AND WHEN A DOG TALKS IN ITS SLEEP.

What type of girl do you like?
ALL OF THEM, OF COURSE! BUT MY VERY FAVORITE ARE THE FIRM AND KIND ONES.

And what do you hate to do?
STUDY. GETTING UP EARLY. HUMID DAYS. AND... KILLING PEOPLE.

What about food?
I EAT ANYTHING! BUT I DON'T LIKE ALCOHOL OR TOBACCO VERY MUCH.

Is there anything that frightens you?
OH, SURE! YUYA-SAN! SHE'S ALWAYS ANGRY WHEN I FINISH THE SNACKS. BUT SHE EATS TWICE AS MUCH AS I DO!

Anything you want to add?
I HAVEN'T BEEN IN THE STORY LATELY, BUT PLEASE DON'T FORGET ME! WHAT? A SUPER-CURLY HAIR STICKING OUT?! I DON'T HAVE THAT! I'M THE MAIN CHARACTER! THE HERO!

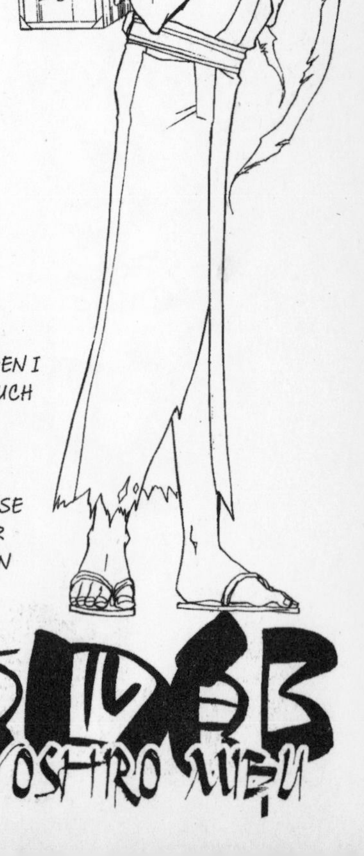

CHARACTER PROFILE

Please introduce yourself.
I'M DEMON EYES KYO. I'VE FORSAKEN MY BIRTH NAME. MY AGE? NONE OF YOUR DAMN BUSINESS. 6', 66KG, BLOOD TYPE B...ORIGINALLY. OCCUPATION?! GO FIGURE IT OUT.

Yes. I'd say samurai. What are some of your favorite things?
ALCOHOL. TOBACCO. WOMEN. AND...KILLING PEOPLE.

Ah-heh-heh...You're joking. (Right?) What about food?
I DON'T EAT WHEN I DRINK ALCOHOL.

Isn't that bad for your liver? Heh-heh. So...uh...what things do you hate?
KYOSHIRO. I HATE THAT BASTARD. HIM...AND WOMEN WHO WEAR TOO MUCH MAKE-UP.

What kind of women do you like? I'd guess an attractive one with a nice figure. Or, maybe, Sakuya-san?
NONE OF YOUR BUSINESS.

I'm sorry! Uh...does anything frighten you?
NOTHING, IDIOT.

Heh-heh-heh...uh...do you have any hobbies or special skills?
I PLAY CHESS. AND I HAVE ONE VERY SPECIAL SKILL. I CAN MAKE SMOKE RINGS WHEN I SMOKE.

My, what an...interesting skill. Heh-heh-heh—gyah! I'm sorry! Uh...any last words?
ANYONE WHO HAS A COMPLAINT, COME SEE ME. I'LL KILL YOU.

Challenge Akimine Kamijyo!

[Akita prefecture/Iruya Nagakura]

VERY DETAILED!

[Hyogo prefecture/ Tomoko Ishibashi]

THEY HAVE SUCH WARM EXPRESSIONS.

Thanks everybody!

You better draw me beautiful!

Did anyone draw me?

I wonder who won this tough challenge?

Cheer up postcard from Mashima sensei, creator of Rave Master.

PLUE IS A GUARDIAN WHO WATCHES OVER MY WORK FROM A HIGHER PLACE.

[Kyoto/Chuta]

DON'T DROP HER, KYO-SHIRO! SHE'LL KILL YOU!

[Fukushima prefecture/ Yoshitaka Sasaki]

THIS IS QUITE A THREESOME!

[Tochigi prefecture/Ferrari]

COOL! BUT WHERE IS THE REST OF THE SWORD?

EXTRA!

[Saitama prefecture/ Matsuo family's little girl]

VERY GOOD! WELL DONE!

MESSAGE FROM AKIMINE KAMIJYO!

LET YOUR PERSONALITY EXPLODE! CHALLENGE ME ANY TIME WITH YOUR OWN KYO!

ENTER NOW!

Send us your illustrations of Kyo characters! The best illustrations will be published in a future volume of Samurai Deeper Kyo.

- Send your questions and comments as well.

[Address] Samurai Deeper KYO fan mail
TOKYOPOP
5900 Wilshire Blvd., Ste 2000,
Los Angeles, CA 90036

Angel G.
aka Sapphire Blaze
Fort Worth, TX

Shuuki
Age: 25

Christine G. Age: 16
Medical Lake, WA

Aimee G.

Yuya

Nicole W.
Wapwallopen, PA

WANT TO EARN
1MILLION
RYO?

John B.
Brunswick, GA

GLOSSARY

Edo—The new capital of Japan after Sekigahara, where the Shogun resides. Present-day Tokyo. To keep better control of the Daimyo (feudal lords), the shogun required that they spend every other year residing in Edo. With so much power centralized there, Edo quickly became one of the worlds' great cities.

Edo Era—(1603-1868) Japan's "golden era" of political and economic stability after the civil wars of the Sengogu Era. Samurai Deeper Kyo takes place at the start of the Edo Era.

Ieyasu Tokugawa—The historical first Shogun. Certain...liberties...have been taken with his role in Samurai Deeper Kyo.

Kansai-ben—Benitora speaks in Kansai-ben, the fast-paced and slangy dialect from Japan's Kansai region (Kobe, Kyoto, Osaka). His way of calling people "-han" instead of "-san" is a trait of that dialect.

Mon—a small silver or copper coin.

Ryo—A gold coin of about 15 grams.

Sekigahara—The greatest battle in Japanese history, it took place in the fall of 1600 and ended the years of civil war in Japan. Following Sekigahara, Japan would be ruled by one Shogun.

Sengoku Era—A time of civil war in Japan which lasted from 1467-1568. It was a warlike age—the heyday of the Samurai.

Shogun—the supreme ruler during Edo Japan.

Honorifics

Samurai Deeper Kyo retains the name suffixes from the original Japanese. In Japanese language there are a number of suffixes (also called honorifics) that come after names and indicate a level of respect between two people. Here is a list of the honorifics you'll see in Samurai Deeper Kyo:

-san—The most common suffix. The equivalent of Mr. or Mrs.

-sama—Indicates great respect or admiration. Used towards people much older or of higher standing.

-chan—Indicates friendly familiarity. Chan is usually applied to girls, but can be used with boys as well.

-dono—Indicates great respect and familiarity. Equivalent to "sir" or "master."

SAMURAI DEEPER KYO NEXT!

The location of Kyo's body is revealed!

Don't miss the astonishing fifth volume! Be ready!

COMING TO EARTH MARCH 2004

ALSO AVAILABLE FROM 

REALITY CHECK
REBIRTH
REBOUND
REMOTE June 2004
RISING STARS OF MANGA December 2003
SABER MARIONETTE J
SAILOR MOON
SAINT TAIL
SAIYUKI
SAMURAI DEEPER KYO
SAMURAI GIRL REAL BOUT HIGH SCHOOL
SCRYED
SGT. FROG March 2004
SHAOLIN SISTERS
SHIRAHIME-SYO: SNOW GODDESS TALES December 2004
SHUTTERBOX
SNOW DROP January 2004
SOKORA REFUGEES May 2004
SORCEROR HUNTERS
SUIKODEN May 2004
SUKI February 2004
THE CANDIDATE FOR GODDESS April 2004
THE DEMON ORORON April 2004
THE LEGEND OF CHUN HYANG
THE SKULL MAN
THE VISION OF ESCAFLOWNE
TOKYO MEW MEW
TREASURE CHESS March 2004
UNDER THE GLASS MOON
VAMPIRE GAME
WILD ACT
WISH
WORLD OF HARTZ
X-DAY
ZODIAC P.I.

NOVELS

KARMA CLUB APRIL 2004
SAILOR MOON

ART BOOKS

CARDCAPTOR SAKURA
MAGIC KNIGHT RAYEARTH
PEACH GIRL ART BOOK January 2004

ANIME GUIDES

COWBOY BEBOP ANIME GUIDES
GUNDAM TECHNICAL MANUALS
SAILOR MOON SCOUT GUIDES

CINE-MANGA™

CARDCAPTORS
FAIRLY ODD PARENTS MARCH 2004
FINDING NEMO
G.I. JOE SPY TROOPS
JACKIE CHAN ADVENTURES
KIM POSSIBLE
LIZZIE MCGUIRE
POWER RANGERS: NINJA STORM
SPONGEBOB SQUAREPANTS
SPY KIDS
SPY KIDS 3-D March 2004
THE ADVENTURES OF JIMMY NEUTRON: BOY GENIUS
TRANSFORMERS: ARMADA
TRANSFORMERS: ENERGON May 2004

TOKYOPOP KIDS

STRAY SHEEP

For more information visit www.TOKYOPOP.com

10103

STOP!

This is the back of the book.
You wouldn't want to spoil a great ending!

This book is printed "manga-style," in the authentic Japanese right-to-left format. Since none of the artwork has been flipped or altered, readers get to experience the story just as the creator intended. You've been asking for it, so TOKYOPOP® delivered: authentic, hot-off-the-press, and far more fun!

DIRECTIONS

If this is your first time reading manga-style, here's a quick guide to help you understand how it works.

It's easy... just start in the top right panel and follow the numbers. Have fun, and look for more 100% authentic manga from TOKYOPOP®!